Making a Short Speech or Toast

JACKIE ARNOLD

A How To Book

ROBINSON

ROBINSON

First published in Great Britain in 2007 by How To Books
This edition published in Great Britain in 2016 by Robinson

NOTE: The material contained is for general guidance and does not deal with particular
circumstances. Laws and regulations are complex and liable to change, and readers should
check the current position with relevant authorities or consult appropriate financial advisers
before making personal arrangements.

A CIP catalogue record for this book is available from the British Library.

ISBN 978-1-47213-639-8 (paperback)

Typeset by SX Composing DTP, Rayleigh, Essex
Printed and bound in Great Britain by CPI Group (UK) Ltd, Croydon, CR0 4YY
Papers used by Rob   and other environmental sources

How To Books are published by Robinson, an imprint of Little, Brown Book Group. We welcome
proposals from authors who have first-hand experience of their subjects. Please set out the aims of your
book, its target market and its suggested contents in an email to Nikki.Read@howtobooks.co.uk

Contents

Introduction

I think the first time I heard a toast being offered was when I was about ten years old and my father stood up at a Christmas dinner and said 'to my wonderful wife who has put up with me for so long'.

I thought that this was a very appropriate thing to say considering the way my father often made less than complimentary comments when she had worked all day in the kitchen, especially at Christmas. I felt that this was his way of saying how much he appreciated her, even if it was a backhanded compliment!

My next memory is of my grandmother Gay, who was a keen bridge player. She used to play on a regular basis and there was always a bottle of dry sherry on the table. I remember her proposing a toast at the start of a game with 'to a handful of trumps and a run of good luck'. She was always coming up with a quote or toast for every occasion and some she passed to me. I remember one in particular when, before drinking her daily glass of sherry, she would raise her glass and say 'a little of what you fancy does you good' and as she finished a glass or two of sherry and some pieces of cheese she made a polite burp followed by 'Pardon me for being so rude it was not me it was my food'.

My family were, it seemed, quite fond of toasting and I felt it was a fun way to start a meal, although strangely enough in my teens and twenties I was one of the only members of my family not to like alcohol. Today things are different and I regularly enjoy a glass of wine with my meal and the occasional vodka and orange.

My father's family came from Scotland and my paternal grandmother was directly descended from the Erskine family, whose ancestors lived in Breamar Castle near St Andrews Bay.

The Scots are great lovers of the toast and Scotland is very famous for its whisky production in addition to the famous Scottish ale. A Scottish toast:

> *May the best you've ever seen,*
> *Be the worst you'll ever see.*

A traditional Scottish horsemen's toast goes:

> *Here's to the horse wi' the four white feet,*
> *The chestnut tail and mane,*
> *A star on his face and a spot on his breast,*
> *An' his master's name was Cain.*

Of course the toast is alive and well in Ireland where the tradition has not been lost and where every pub reverberates to the sound of clinking glasses. Very often a toast in Ireland will be referred to as a 'blessing'. Here are a few examples.

Health and long life to you
The wife of your choice to you
Land free of rent to you
From this day forth

May you have warm words on a cold evening
A full moon on a dark night
And the road downhill all the way to your door.

May the road rise to meet you
May the wind be always at your back
The sun shine warm on your face
The rain fall soft upon your fields
And until we meet again
May God hold you in the hollow of his hand.

This latter toast is very familiar and is often given to guests when they leave an Irish home. You may also see this on the wall of an Irish pub to wish you well. The Irish are very hospitable and have many toasts of welcome and goodwill.

Of course Wales is the land of song and they also have a long tradition of toasting particularly with beer and cider, for example:

To the land we love and the love we land.

In 2000 I was looking for a speakers club in Brighton as I wanted to improve my confidence in front of larger audiences. I searched in vain and then someone suggested I visit a Toastmasters Club. 'Well, I am not looking to be a toastmaster' I thought, but my colleague explained that the International Toastmaster Clubs provide great training in public speaking and really encouraged me to go along. My first visit was to Chichester where the club was very professional and actually quite formal. I was not sure if this was what I was looking for, but the whole evening was very informative and I learnt a lot. I decided to visit two more clubs, one in Guildford and another in London, to see what they offered. I was amazed at the array of skills it was possible to learn. Not only did they have a complete educational programme for public speaking, but also for leadership and advanced communication.

I immediately decided to start a toastmasters club in Brighton and Hove and in June 2001 we were a fully chartered club with twenty-five paid up members. Today the club is thriving and after a successful fifteen years is going from strength to strength.

What's in the Book

I have researched the toasts in this book by asking friends, foreign students and work colleagues to contribute. In Chapter 2 you will find guidelines on how to prepare and deliver a mini speech with examples on structure, planning and nerve-busting techniques. There are foreign expressions and quotes to insert if you are visiting another country and want to say a few words.

For example in China *Ganbei* usually means 'down the hatch' (literally to drink the entire glass full) so to be sure it is necessary to watch the person offering the toast to see if he/she drinks all the contents.

In the section on humorous toasts in Chapter 5, I have included many ideas from friends as to how they used humour to good effect, as in this example:

> *As you slide down the banister of life,*
> *may the splinters never point the wrong way.*

There are also guidelines on how to introduce humour and how to avoid embarrassing your audience inappropriately.

In the wedding section in Chapter 6 I have drawn from other best man's and groom's speeches I have heard and enjoyed, and there are several interesting quotes and toasts for you to insert into your wedding speech, such as:

May 'for better or worse' be far better than worse!

There are tips for the father of the bride and a section on etiquette plus advice on what not to say! If you are nervous about standing up in front of an audience there are also useful tips to help you plan, deliver and gain confidence as a speaker.

At the end of the book I have included a workbook section where you can glean ideas on appropriate beginnings and endings to speeches, and where you can plan your ideas and toasting expressions. There are proverbs and limericks to add colour to your speeches and even guidelines on how to write your own. I have also consulted many books and found several gems (with permission) on the internet. Wherever possible I have given the source and name of the person quoted. There are many whose source is not known. Some of the toasts (including the one below) and quotes are my own. I hope you enjoy them.

Do you enjoy good food and wine? Then raise your glass and toast
Hear phrases trickle through your mind
From foreign shores to the British coast

Raise your glass to celebrate
Let us this moment seize
Friends, relations gather round and
Raise your glasses, please!

1. Wherefore the Toast? A Bit of History

If all be true that I do think
There are five reasons we should drink:
Good wine – a friend – or being dry –
Or if we should be by and by –
Or any other reason why!

Henry Aldrich (1710)

In the Beginning ...

Raising a glass to a great cause or simply to honour good friends is a tradition in every country in the world, or at least every country I can think of. Though the words may differ and the period of oration may vary from a few seconds to a few minutes, the fundamental reason for toasting is the same: to celebrate as a group.

But where did this custom come from? And why is the word for this social ritual the same as a roasted piece of bread? In the book *Panati's Extraordinary Origins of Everyday Things*, Charles Panati writes that the actual act of drinking to a guest's health or good fortune started in ancient Greece. The host would drink first to demonstrate that his wine was not poisoned, a practice which had become quite a common way of dealing with rivals, competitors, or no-longer-wanted spouses. Over time, the sequence of host drinking first followed by guests came to be considered an act that symbolised friendship and goodwill. Other sources have noted that another reason for a group glass raising was the pledge of three cups – one each to Mercury, the Graces and Zeus.

Why 'toasting'?

Panati writes that the Romans took up the practice of toasting (and poisoning) from the Greeks, and added the custom of dropping a piece of charred bread into the cup. Charcoal has been shown to reduce acidity in a liquid, so one assumes that the Romans used this as a means of mellowing the taste of low-quality, vinegary wine. It is from this practice that we come by the term 'toast' – from the Latin word *tostus*, which means roasted, though its use to signify a raising of glasses was apparently not common until the seventeenth century.

An ancient Persian legend states how wine was discovered.

Prince Jemshed ordered some goatskin bags to be labelled 'poison' after the fermenting grape juice in them gave him a stomach ache. His once favourite wife, having lost his favour, decided to kill herself by drinking some of the liquid from the bags. Unbeknown to her the wine had matured, and she became happy and flirtatious again. The result was that she won back the favour of her husband, who realised that the 'wine' was far from poison.

Wine and cocktails

Wine was introduced into Northern Europe about 600 BC and was always 'still' after maturing because it was brewed in open vessels. It was only in the late seventeenth century that corks were introduced by a Benedictine monk, Don Perignon, and this introduction of a leakproof stopper meant that secondary fermentation could take place, putting bubbles into the champagne-type wines sold today.

The cocktail was apparently first drunk in the days of cock fighting as a toast to the cock who had the most tail feathers left after a battle. The theory that it was called after *a couqetier*, a type of French cup in which it was served, is a more palatable explanation today. Another idea is that it comes from *coquetel*, a mixed drink from the wine region of Gironde which is said to have been popular during the French Revolution.

The Lord's Hall

Toasting came in very handy in the Middle Ages. The feudal lord oversaw the principal meal of his household in the great hall of his castle. After the meal was complete he signalled for talk, music, or story, the latter often requested of guests to the table.

Seated at the head of the table the lord made the opening speech, an address of welcome. This might be very brief or quite lengthy.

It might pledge an attentive and courteous hearing to whatever story the guest would be telling, it might refer to the past glory of the castle and its lord, or it might boast of present greatness. At the end of this monologue, the lord raised his glass and called for a communal drink of goodwill and friendship.

The guest was then expected to respond in kind, either before or after entertaining those assembled with his story. Again, glasses were raised and everyone's health was drunk. This process would be repeated over and over by host, guest, and other members of the household, often for many hours.

Making the evening interesting

When no guests sat at the table, the need for toasting was even greater. Among a group that lived under the same roof day in and day out, things could get, well, boring. As the last thing our lord wanted was a dull evening, he introduced the toast to inject energy into the proceedings. He might himself propose a toast of his own choice or give someone else permission to propose it. A compliment, a proverb, or a speech and a response, however bawdy, got and kept the attention of everyone at the table. While the lord as host would start things off, he most likely gave permission or invitation to others at the table to follow suit. As in the case of meals with guests, the toasts might go on for hours.

Today our stories are shorter and the number of toasts we propose at one sitting tends to be fewer, but the toasting tradition we carry forward has roots in those days of lords, castles and great halls.

Bits and Pieces of Toasting Lore

Anecdotes and stories about toasting abound, some true, some not, some hard to verify one way or the other. Here are some items that might simply be of interest, or that may come in handy the next time your cocktail conversation turns to the toast.

Anatomy of a toast

No matter how short or long, how formal or informal, a toast consists of three parts.

1. The toast itself, where one person states the reason for the toast.

2. The agreement, where everyone present signifies agreement by lifting drinks into the air, making loud or soft sounds of agreement such as 'hear hear!', and clinking glasses against those of anyone within reach.

3. The symbolic drink, a quick sip or a long draught as desired, to confirm the agreement.

A touch of the macabre

In his book *A Brief History of the Raised Glass*, Paul Dickson notes that in earlier days the Scots and Scandinavians drank from the skulls of fallen enemies. This practice is said to be the source of the standard Scandinavian *skoal*, which is an abbreviation of *ta för er ur skoalen*, which means 'help yourself from the drinking vessel'!

The Danish had a nasty habit of cutting the throats of Britons while they were drinking. This practice led to the habit of drinking to someone's health – if I drank to your health, it meant that I would guard your throat while you drink to keep you alive.

Don't duel, drink

In the 1600s men routinely carried a sword, dagger, or other weapon with them, usually on the right side. Raising a glass in the right hand, therefore, was considered an act of friendship.

Clinking: pick your preference!

There seem to be several schools of thought around why we clink classes during the second part of a toast. Some say that it goes back to the pesky concern about poisoning. In those bad old days, toasters went further than simply clinking – they actually poured a bit of their wine into their friend's cup. The idea was that if there's poison in my cup, now there's poison in yours, and we're both going to kick the bucket. As time went on and poisoning went out of fashion, this custom devolved to merely clinking rims.

Another reason cited by some is that the noise of the clinking – simulating the sound of a bell – would scare away demons and devils.

Finally there is the explanation that when we sniff, swirl and swallow wine it offers pleasures to four of the five senses. The only missing sense is hearing, hence the addition of the clink.

They thought it was the toast, not the beverage

It might be difficult to fathom today, but toasting once received at least as much blame for degenerating society as alcohol itself. One of the primary goals of the first temperance society, formed in the early sixteenth century, was to abolish the practice of toasting. Toasting had become so frequent in the seventeenth and eighteenth centuries – thus leading to intoxication and all the behaviours attached to that state – that various monarchs of England and France (including Louis XIV) decided to ban the practice of toasting, but as we know, the ban didn't stick.

Toast of the town

Charles Panati includes a charming bit of toasting history in his book. In early eighteenth-century England, gentlemen dining together would drink the health of a particularly beautiful woman who was not present at the dinner. Acquaintance with the lady in question was not a requirement; apparently the only thing needed was universal agreement about her beauty. This practice became so widely used that a lady who garnered this kind of attention came to be called a 'toast of the town'.

How to win enemies

In nineteenth-century England toasting someone at the table with every glass, and there were often many glasses drunk, became the norm. One sure way to insult a person in this era was to fail to toast him or her during the meal.

The immortal memory

Remembering Vice-Admiral Horatio Lord Nelson in a special toast called The Immortal Memory at Trafalgar Day dinner was a general practice by the mid-nineteenth century. This event celebrated Nelson's 1805 victory, and his death, at the Battle of Trafalgar during England's war with Napoleon. Though the custom dwindled after the First World War when Armistice Day was established to honour all the country's war veterans, the Royal Navy still drinks to 'the immortal memory of Nelson' at the annual dinner aboard the HMS *Victory* on Trafalgar Day. HMS *Victory* is the oldest naval ship still in commission and the only remaining ship of the line of the Royal Navy, now in dry dock in Portsmouth as a museum ship.

This particular toast is one instance where there is no verbal agreement by the drinkers after the toast is made. Instead, the toast is drunk standing in total silence.

Anything but water!

A Navy tradition demands that a toast never be made with water. The reason for this taboo is that a person so honoured will be doomed to a watery grave. Whether for this reason or some other source, in general it is considered bad luck to toast with water. Some etiquette watchdogs also say it's 'not done' to toast with coffee or tea, though other non-alcoholic beverages are quite acceptable.

Toasting without the Graeco-Roman roots

In the South Pacific natives of Fiji drink a narcotic drink known as *kava*, a substance that numbs the tongue and lips. They have an elaborate ceremony around the drinking of *kava*, and non-native visitors are invited to partake in an abbreviated form of the rituals. Guests are required to bring a gift of *kava* roots, and speeches are required from everyone, even if there is nothing to say other than 'I came because I want to try *kava*'. All in attendance clap once before drinking and three times afterwards. A drinker must finish the entire cup, even if they don't like it, which is not unusual for non-Fijians.

One-ups-man statesmanship

While Benjamin Franklin was the American emissary to France in the latter part of the eighteenth century, an occasion for a toast took on a bit of a competitive air. The British Ambassador led off with 'to George the Third, who, like the sun in its meridian, spreads lustre throughout and enlightens the world'.

Obligated to follow suit, the French minister took up the challenge with, 'to the illustrious Louis XVI, who, like the moon, sheds his benevolent rays on and influences the globe'.

Finally, Franklin rose and lifted his glass. His response: 'to George Washington, commander of the American armies, who, like Joshua of old, commanded the sun and moon to stand still and both obeyed'.

Unfortunately, in the latter part of the twentieth century, diplomatic toasting took an even worse turn. There have been several instances at state dinners where a 'toast' was a thinly veiled political speech or, worse, an insult.

'Here's mud in yer eye!'

Though today this toast is associated with films of the old American West, it was actually originated by farmers to express their desire that the soil they ploughed would be soft.

'Here we come, a-being of health!'

The word wassail derives from the first recorded toast in England. The story goes that King Vortigern hosted a feast for Saxon leader Hengist and his entourage. During the feast, Hengist's daughter Rowena raised her goblet and said, 'Louerd King, waes hael!' which means 'Lord King, be of health!' The King replied, 'drink, hael.' The 'waes-hael/drink-hael' exchange became the common toast for many centuries.

By the seventeenth century, the first part of the toast had become quite specific, both to a particular beverage and a particular time of year, when people went from house to house with their empty wassail bowls offering to sing Christmas carols for a bit of the spiced brew.

Did they think no one noticed?

Jacobites in England would secretly toast their exiled prince by passing their glass over a container of water as they participated in a toast to King George – so that they were actually toasting to 'the king across the water'.

An interesting pedigree

At the beginning of the nineteenth century an enthusiastic London drinking club met regularly at the Crown and Anchor tavern. Named for the Greek poet Anacreon, the Anacreontic Society always opened their meetings by singing a toast 'to Anacreon in Heaven'. The song presumably was heard by American visitors, either at the meetings themselves or elsewhere in the city, and it was thus carried across the Atlantic. Following the custom of applying different lyrics to catchy tunes, the melody of this toast was applied to different lyrics – most notably by an American named Francis Scott Key for his poem *Star-Spangled Banner*.

Pub toasts

Today a lot of the toasting goes on in pubs, the shortened version of public house. If they call it a free house this means they can sell any type of beer like Wadworth, Youngs, Harveys, Speckled Hen, etc … It depends on which part of the UK you live in as many breweries are local. If the pub sells draught beer this is beer sold at a pump 'on draught' and this is where the expression 'pull a pint' comes from. A stout is usually Guinness and stouts are mainly from Ireland.

Toasts are generally made after a 'round of drinks' has been made and everyone has a glass. People buy a round or stand a round by saying 'my shout' or 'my round'. Sometimes you will hear 'what's yours?' or 'what'll you have?' Sometimes if someone has forgotten they'll be reminded by 'hey, it's your round!'

Some modern toasts heard in pubs are:

Cheers
Down the hatch
Your good health
Here's to you
Get that down you
Bottoms up
Eat, drink and be merry.

The Birth of the Toastmaster

The practice of toasting became so prevalent and so much a part of socialising in the eighteenth and nineteenth centuries that it could take hours. The Scandinavians drank to absent friends, a practice that was enthusiastically adopted and that lengthened the proceedings even further. Eventually, the role of toastmaster evolved. A toastmaster's job was to propose toasts, announce toasts, and make sure that everyone who wanted to make a toast was given an opportunity to do so. He was also required to stay sober and make sure that no offence was given during the proceedings.

Today there are experts who take on the mantle of toastmaster at weddings and celebrations. If you are part of the family or an invited guest you do not want to be organising the structure of the day and the toastmaster can very effectively do this for you. Many hotels and wedding planners include this service as part of their wedding package.

The modern toastmaster

Gloria Sweden lives in London and is a Lady Toastmaster. She started life as a singer and cabaret artist and it was while singing karaoke and doing some announcements that she was approached and asked if she would like to become a Lady Toastmaster. The training, through the Institute of Toastmasters, is quite thorough as it is necessary to know how to address people appropriately, the correct etiquette for many different occasions and how to perform your duties at weddings of various denominations. There are two final exams, one oral and one written, which are taken after the first six months. Then it is necessary to shadow a trained Toastmaster until you are confident and able to work on your own.

Gloria lists the following skills and attributes as being essential for the role of Toastmaster.

• Caring about people and wanting to support them.

• Having a laid-back and relaxed approach, particularly when things go wrong.

• Being diplomatic and understanding, and willing to serve people and make their day special.

She has on a couple of occasions needed quick reactions when the wedding gifts went missing and the bride's dress was torn. She tells us that it is important to have a good balance between ensuring that all the arrangements and speeches run smoothly and being unobtrusive.

Gloria explains that the modern role of Toastmaster is to adapt to the requirements of the couples concerned. Today many couples get married in the same venue as the reception, or have a simple civic marriage with a few drinks afterwards. Under these circumstances she is called upon to act less formally than at a large church wedding with separate reception and dinner dance.

After introducing any speeches the Toastmaster will help to arrange the cutting of the cake and will be on hand to make sure that the guests are served and to assist the bride and groom where necessary.

Generally she wears her full uniform, which can cost as much as £600 a time, the red jacket being the most distinctive and most expensive item. At less formal occasions she can be asked to wear a black suit to blend easily into the background.

Gloria's past experience as a singer has allowed her to be able to make the announcements sound interesting and lively, 'ladies and gentlemen, please stand for the bride and groom', 'ladies and gentlemen, please take your seats for the wedding supper' and so on. Being able to speak slowly and with clear diction is vitally important as many people will be talking and it is often difficult to be heard above the noise in the room. She uses a presentation style of speaking, and rehearses and prepares just as an actor would prepare for a role, while remaining natural, and in her words 'treating every occasion as if it were your own and never forgetting to smile'.

Often Toastmasters are asked to be even more involved and help to organise the gifts, pin on the buttonholes, and in an emergency be the person who 'saves the day'.

Gloria told me a story of when the bride had left all the wedding presents in her office and then it fell on the Toastmaster to make sure someone (in this case the DJ who was available) drove quickly to the office and collected the gifts so that they could be laid out on the table.

It seems that not only do Toastmasters fill the role of announcer and presenter, but also they are the main person who sees that the whole day runs smoothly and effectively, whatever the occasion. Ladies' nights, civil receptions, formal dinners, golfing functions and so on are other occasions where a Toastmaster's skills are called upon. Gloria is a very successful Lady Toastmaster and has made an interesting and varied career in what is generally considered to be a male dominated role.

Public speaking clubs worldwide known as Toastmasters International

The term Toastmasters International should not be confused with the role of Toastmaster above. They are public speaking clubs where members are mentored and encouraged to further their self-development in communication and leadership.

The first club was formed in October 1924, when a group of men assembled by Dr Ralph C. Smedley met in the basement of the Santa Ana, California, YMCA to form a club 'to afford practice and training in the art of public speaking and in presiding over meetings, and to promote sociability and good fellowship among its members'. The group took the name Toastmasters.

New programmes, including the Advanced Communication and Leadership Programmes, Success/Leadership Series, and self-study cassette tapes, were later added. The training, support and highly effective mentoring that members receive are second to none. It is interesting to note that, on average, the gross membership of Toastmasters International increases at a rate of approximately 250 people per day. Currently there are over 10,500 clubs and more than 200,000 members in approximately 90 countries.

In 2001 I set up Brighton and Hove Speakers Club in the UK and chartered it the same month under the Toastmasters International banner. In 2006 three more clubs were set up on the Sussex coast.

Honing your public speaking

At very little cost these clubs help to foster a safe and supportive environment to hone the art of public speaking and leadership. If you are looking to find a safe environment in which to practice your speeches the Toastmaster speakers clubs are fun, informative and amazingly cheap. A colleague who joined our local club put it very well.

> I joined the local speakers club as I was not comfortable speaking to large groups of people. What I learnt enabled me to change the way I managed people in a variety of situations, not only at business meetings, but also one to one. This year I gave a successful short speech at my daughter's wedding so all in all it was a *highly* valuable experience.

Toastmaster speaking competitions are run all over the country in each area, district and then nationally. The national winners then have the opportunity to travel to the USA, where they will be up against speakers from all over the world. The annual conferences are a true testimony to the success of these clubs as there are highly motivational workshops, and an opportunity to step up and speak to several hundred people for the first time.

> *The greatest mistake you can make in life is to be continually fearing that you will make one.*
> Ellen Hubbard

> *Look like today, speak like today, use today's stories and you will be thought of as today's speaker.*
> Doug Malouf

> *A toast to enthusiasm – for 15% of speaking success is due to knowledge, **and 85%** from enthusiasm!*
> Adapted from Stanford University study

See page 134 for further details and how to join a TM speakers club.

2. Toasts and Short Speeches

General Guidelines

Raise your glass to the present moment. The past is history, the future's a mystery, and today is a gift – that's why it's called the present.
Babatunde Olatunji

Throw off the bowlines. Sail away from the safe harbour. Catch the trade winds in your sails. Explore. Dream. Discover.
Mark Twain

Here's to life – for ... life is like an onion: you peel it off one layer at a time, and sometimes you weep.
Karl Sandburg

Though the practice of toasting is nowhere near as extensive or inebriating as it once was, toasts are still very much a part of special occasions in our lives – anniversaries, birthdays, engagements, graduation, launch parties, new job, prize-giving, promotion, reunions, holidays, weddings, or simply good times with good friends.

Formal Toasting Etiquette

At formal occasions such as banquets and receptions the host or hostess offers the first toast. While he or she stands, everyone else – including the person being toasted – remains seated unless the toaster requests otherwise.

The preamble list depends on who is present on the occasion – here are some general guidelines on how to address people at formal functions.

- With the exception of 'may it please Your Majesty' if the Queen is present the preamble will begin with the host (if the speaker is not the host – in which case he/she will not include him/herself).

- The host is addressed by his/her title such as: Mr/Madam President, Mr/Madam Chairman, Mr/Madam Vice Chancellor and so on.

- A member of the Royal family standing as President would be addressed as 'Your Royal Highness and President' and 'Your Grace' covers Dukes and Duchesses.

- High Commissioners and Ambassadors are addressed as 'Your Excellency'.

After the preamble the toaster will say:

Ladies and gentlemen, please stand and raise your glass to …

or

> *Ladies and gentlemen, pray silence for a toast to ...*

The person to whom the toast is directed neither stands nor drinks. Once the toast is finished, they smile acknowledgement and say thank you. At this point they may elect to rise and propose a toast of their own to the host and anyone else they want to honour.

Informal Toasting Etiquette

> *To life:*
> *Life is a jest, and all things show it*
> *I thought so once but now I know it.*
> John Gay 1685–1732

Informal occasions are much less structured. At a small gathering of family or friends, someone other than the host may initiate the toasting. Often, in fact, the first toast acknowledges and thanks the host for their hospitality. There is no need for the toaster to rise in these instances, though they can certainly do so if desired.

The person proposing the toast will generally say something along the lines of:

> *I'd like to propose a toast to (name).*

Followed by a very brief reason such as ...

> *for his/her wonderful achievement/on this special birthday*
> *occasion/in honour of his/her great contribution to ...* and
> so on.

There are a variety of toasting words and phrases such as:

Cheers
Good luck
Well done
Here's to you
Down the hatch
Bottoms up
Here's mud in yer eye (hoping people would get a safe carriage home)
Break a leg (for actors about to go on stage)
The French 'bon voyage' for a safe journey
'To your new life' for those emigrating.

Other occasions demanding a less formal toast
(See also toasts from A–Z, Chapter 7)

• Before a special dinner with friends

The food is arriving we all have our wine
So raise up your glass and friends let us dine!

• After the party/dinner

We thank you for the food and drink
For the company and the wine
We thank you for the laughter
We've had a brilliant time.

Quick Look Toasting Guidelines
Here are toasting guidelines that work in pretty much any situation.

• When dining in a group, do not drink or propose a toast until everyone has been served their beverage. Also, do not drink until after a toast is made.

- Don't jump ahead of the host unless you know it will be acceptable. If you do want to propose a toast and don't know what the host plans, ask his or her permission before giving the first toast.

- If you wish to propose a toast in a large gathering, stand up and get the group's attention. The days are gone when standing on your chair was the thing to do for this. Simply stand and be patient; people will notice you and quieten their neighbours down. Refrain from tapping the edge of your glass to get people's attention; this is considered tacky and potentially damaging to fine glassware. Don't start your toast until everyone is quiet, and take your time during delivery.

- When possible, include more than one person in your toast. Raise your glass to a couple, a family, a team, a class, or whatever group is involved in your social event.

- Speak to everyone, not just a small group of people. Speak loud enough so that everyone can hear.

- In spite of toasting history, alcohol is no longer the centre of the ritual. Being a teetotaller doesn't excuse you from proposing or participating in toasts. If you don't drink alcohol, you can toast with any potable liquid, though water, coffee and tea are discouraged by some.

- Whether proposing a toast or participating in someone else's, try to make eye contact with others when clinking glasses, but don't make a production of it. Some cultures are earnest about doing the eye thing, others don't do it, and still others can go one way or the other.

- Make the clink gentle to protect the glassware.

- Sip your drink at the end of the toast, don't gulp. And do be sure to take a sip before setting your glass down.

- Never toast with an empty glass.

- Stay sober – at least until your own toast has been delivered.

- This should go without saying, but I will say it anyway: Don't toast yourself. Ever.

Short Speeches

Sometimes an occasion will call for a slightly longer speech. This can occur when thanking people for long service in a company or when giving a political or military toast. Here are some tips for planning, preparing and practising (the three PPPs) for the occasion.

Planning

> *I keep six honest serving men, they taught me all I knew.*
> *Their names are What and Why and When, and How and*
> *Where and Who.*
> Rudyard Kipling

- **What** is the occasion and what key points do you want to include?

  Here you decide what is appropriate for the occasion. Can you bring in a little humour or is it a more serious speech? What key points would be relevant and useful? Think about what the audience want to hear and take away. Often three main points broken down into three smaller points is an effective way to start.

- **Why** is the occasion special and why is the person/are the people celebrating?

  Identify the unique aspects of the occasion as no two celebrations are the same or with the same people. There will be special reasons, events and personal qualities you need to consider. How can you bring these to life by adding a prop, photo, picture or quote?

- **When** will you need to be ready by and when/how often will you need to practise?

  Think carefully about the timing of the speech and how long in advance you need to plan and practise. For every ten minutes of speech you need an hour of practice at least! When will you gather any props and test the technical equipment?

- **How** will you make an impact and how will you keep their attention?

  Making an impact needs some thought and takes practice. The best way is to weave stories and personal anecdotes into your speech. The audience will then be able to identify with them and feel more involved. Even if your material is dry you can still bring in a human interest story. Keep their attention by asking hypothetical questions, or a 'did you know…' question to retain their interest. Change your position on the stage once or twice and alter your tone and pace as you introduce a new element or story.

- **Where** will the event be held and where will you stand to deliver your speech?

  It is useful to be able to visit the venue ahead of time. Seeing the venue and planning where you will stand will give you confidence as it can then be visualised positively. See yourself giving the speech and visualise your success and the resulting applause – very motivating!

- **Who** will you be addressing and what do you know about them?

  Knowing who you will be addressing can really help with your planning. What/who have they heard before? What do they already know and is there anyone else speaking at this event? Anything you can find out will give you an advantage and help calm your nerves.

- **What** can you do to reduce your nerves?

  Breathing correctly is the key to successful speaking. It serves to calm the nerves beforehand; it enables the brain to function well.

Note that this is often why people lose their way, not because they have forgotten the words, but because they haven't learnt to breathe properly!

Visualising yourself as successful can also help, as can taking the time to pause between points. This gives you and the audience time to engage in the content and absorb what you are saying. Then finally practice, practice and practice.

When planning your speech it is important to be brief and to the point. Choose a maximum of three main points and stick to them.

Preparing

First, prepare the answers to the questions above. Make sure you are focusing on the audience and their needs first. Then prepare yourself by writing down all the times you have spoken in public before. Even if it was only to a few people or when you have made a successful telephone call or had a challenging face-to-face discussion with more than one person. All this experience will give you transferable skills and knowledge you can use for speaking in public or at events. Focus on your strengths and what you did well. How can you apply them to the current situation?

Begin or end with a quote or a little story about the person you are toasting to bring in a human element. Choose from those in this book or use the internet to search for an appropriate quote. Maybe you can bring a prop or photo to emphasise your message. Make sure your speech has these three vital parts.

- **The introduction** – the quote, statement, interesting fact or brief story.

- **The development** – the main ideas and reasons for your toast.

- **The summing up** – an amusing line or observation and the call to toast.

Here is an example from a teachers' dinner before proposing a toast for the teachers in the maths department.

> *This year has been a great success and the computer systems have greatly enhanced the efficiency of the maths department. As I am sure you all know David overcame resistance and scepticism with tact and humour helping us all to accept the changes.*
>
> (Intro with personal anecdote)
>
> *Thank you for your efforts to come to grips with the new technology and I know that this has sometimes been a challenge!*
>
> (Reason for toast)
>
> *In proposing a toast to the whole department I would like to say …*
>
> (Amusing toast)

This is especially appropriate:

> *Now here's to technology –*
> *Another pint, pray!*
> *Then here's to the old ways –*
> *Just take them away!*
> *Here's to advancement –*
> *So fill up with wine!*
> *And here's to persistence –*
> *Let's drink yours and mine!*

Practising

After you have planned and prepared your speech you need to take time to practise. Winston Churchill always used one hour of practice for every minute he spoke. When asked how he always managed to be so spontaneous he replied, 'in order to be spontaneous you need to practise, practise and practise'.

- Write your speech out and ideally record it onto a tape and play it back to yourself as often as possible. The advantage of this method is that the main body of the speech is in your memory and you will not read it word for word.

- Put your ideas in bullet points onto a card as briefly as possible to jog your memory. If you cannot memorise the quote then write it out in full, but try not to read it. Keep eye contact with your audience as much as you can.

- Practise your speech in front of a member of your close friends or family and ask them for honest feedback. Ask them to tell you two things to improve and two things they liked.

- Concentrate on your audience or the person you are toasting. This is for them and it is not about you or how well you perform.

- Be enthusiastic – this is a happy occasion and everyone will take the lead from you.

- Before you stand up centre yourself by taking a deep breath and bring your thoughts and attention to the person/people you are toasting.

So What Do I Say?

Starting your speech/toast

- On behalf of … (if you are speaking for someone else or for your company)

- I/we'd like to say/to begin by saying …

- I have been asked to …

- I am not accustomed to speaking in public so bear with me … (more modern version of 'unaccustomed as I am …')

• May I begin by saying …

• So I'd like to finish by: – proposing a toast to …
                            – thanking …
                            – letting you know that …
                            – asking you to join me in a toast to …

• I'd like to end with a toast to/ a short joke/ a short story …

• So please raise your glasses to …

• Now please stand and join me in a toast to …

• I'd like to propose a toast to …

• Thank you for coming, we wish you a safe journey home. (At your venue.)

• Thank you for inviting us and we hope to see you again soon. (At their venue.)

Customs and Toasts for Different Occasions

Different occasions have different toasting customs. Here are some general examples.

There is a more extensive alphabetical list at the end of the book and more toasts to suit the different occasions in Chapter 7.

Birthday

At a birthday celebration someone is selected to propose a toast to the person whose birthday it is, and then they reply by thanking the guests and those who brought presents.

Toast

Here's to (name) may he/she bear in mind that 'Time is a companion that goes with us on a journey. It reminds us to cherish each moment, because it will never come again. What we leave behind is not as important as how we have lived.'
Patrick Stewart, from the film *Star Trek Generations*

Competition/award winner

Competition wins are always celebrated with some form of toast to the winner and sometimes to the runner-up. Toasts such as 'well done – a fantastic result' or 'to a wonderful achievement – cheers' are commonplace. However it is always extra special if you can find something to say about the particular circumstances surrounding the event or the person, such as the following.

Toast

(Name) has driven us all to distraction over the past few months with her persistence and determination to train effectively for this event and to find sponsorship, but look at the result. Today we have nothing but praise for her great achievement. Please raise your glasses and drink to (name).

Christening

At a christening lunch, toasts are usually proposed to the guest of honour (the child) first by the godparents, followed by parents, siblings and, sometimes, guests.

Toast

I would like to propose a toast to (name) with lines from **Peter Pan:** *'When the first baby laughed for the first time, the laugh broke into a thousand pieces and they all went skipping about, and that was the beginning of the fairies.'*
Here's to a happy baby.

Toast

> To his/her 'health, wealth and happiness'.

Engagement

Traditionally the announcement of an engagement was made by the father of the bride to be to the rest of the family. Today, however, it is often the couple themselves who announce the event to their parents and/or guests. At a family party or dinner to celebrate, the toast is usually made by the father or mother of the bride, and the future son-in-law usually replies by toasting the new parents-in-law and generally adds something complimentary or amusing about his future wife.

Toast to the couple

From a quote by Franklin P. Jones:

> Love doesn't make the world go 'round
> Love is what makes the ride worthwhile.

Funeral

Toasts are given in honour of the deceased at the reception after the funeral. It is usual for the eldest son or daughter, or close relative, to propose the first toast followed by a brief personal reflection on the life of the deceased. At times such as these it is advisable to be brief and to make comments lighthearted. Pick out a happy moment or special event to share with the guests and then ask them to remember the deceased by raising their glasses and drinking a toast.

General blessing

> May the road rise to meet you. May the wind be always at your back.
> May the sun shine warm upon your face, the rains fall soft upon the fields.
> And, until we meet again, may God hold you in the palm of his hand.

Graduation

Graduating from college or university is a special event in anyone's life and is usually celebrated by friends and/or family.

Toast

Here's to (name) for overcoming the obstacles and achieving (degree, award, certificate, diploma) and in the words of Helen Keller 'The richness of the human experience would lose something of rewarding joy if there were no limitations to overcome.' Well done.

Quote

Minds are like parachutes – they only function when open.
Thomas Dewar

Launch party/team success

When launching a new product or service it is customary to hold a launch party to thank those involved and to mention the particular efforts of the people involved. At a recent launch party I overheard the following.

Toast

This year we were brave enough to follow a new idea and see it through to its conclusion. We remembered the words of Alexander Graham Bell when he said that 'When one door closes another door opens; but we so often look so long and so regretfully upon the closed door, that we do not see the ones which open for us.' To the open door and beyond – cheers!

Thank you

There are always reasons to thank people and in today's society the thank you card has been largely replaced by e-mail or telephone. This makes the personal toast all the more special. Saying thank you is not enough so mention the way the gift/act/occasion affected you and why it was special.

George Elliston puts this very well when he writes the following:

Toast

How beautiful a day can be, when kindness touches it!
So … let's propose a toast to the kindness of (name) who by …
(exactly what he did) made this day so special.

Toast

I would thank you from the bottom of my heart, but for you (name)
my heart has no bottom.
Anon.

3. Toasting Around the World

When we drink, we get drunk.
When we get drunk, we fall asleep.
When we fall asleep, we commit no sin.
When we commit no sin, we go to heaven.
So, let's all get drunk, and go to heaven!

While there are many different cultures around the world, all of them have one thing in common: honoured guests are invited to dine. And when humans dine, they often toast. Not all cultures drink alcoholic beverages, but most if not all have some kind of toasting custom.

In fact, raising a glass in convivial company is ubiquitous and quite similar around the globe. Virtually every country has some kind of 'everyday' toast that is used in the majority of situations. English speaking countries uniformly use 'Cheers!' for common usage. Spanish speaking countries generally use 'salud!' or the longer 'salud, amor y pesetas, y el tiempo para disfrutarlos!' ('health, love and money and the time to enjoy them!').

The Most Common Toasts

Following is a list of some (but definitely nowhere near all) of the common toasts in selected countries. As there may be other commonly used words or phrases in specific regions, ask a local ahead of time what the appropriate toast is for the situation you are in.

TOASTING QUICK LIST

Australia	Cheers!
Brazil	Tim-tim!
Canada	Cheers!
China	Gombui! (Cantonese) Ganbei! (Mandarin)
Denmark	Skoal!
England	Cheers!
Finland	Kippis!
France	A votre santé!
	Cul sec! (bottoms up)
	Un repas sans vin, c'est comme un jour sans soleil
	(a meal without wine is like a day without sun)
Germany	Prohst!
Greece	Yasou!
Hebrew	Le'chájim! (*lukh-high-yum*)
India (Hindi)	Mubarik!
Iran	Be Salam ati!
Ireland	Sláinte! (*slawn-chah*)
	Sláinte Mhor! (*slawn-chah more*)
	Go mbeirimíd beo ar an ám seo arís
	(that we may be alive and well this time next year)

	Go neirí an bóthar leat (wherever you go that the wind will always be on your back, ie that you will have good luck and fortune wherever you shall go)
Italy	Salute!
	Cin Cin! (*cheen cheen*)
Japan	Kanpai! (*kam pie*)
New Zealand	Cheers!
	Kia ora (Maori)
Norway	Skoal!
Philippines (Tagalog)	Mabuhay!
Poland	(Na) zdrowie!
Portugal	Saúde!
Rome	Salve!
Russia	Za vashe zdorovie!
Scotland	Sláinte! (*slawn-chah*)
Traditional toast	Lang may yer lum reek!
	Lang may yer lum reek! (Long may your chimney smoke!)
	Wi' ither folks coal. (With other people's coal!)
Burns' Selkirk grace	Some hae meat, and canna eat, And some wad eat that want it; But we hae meat, and we can eat – And sae the Lord be thankit.
Spain	Salud!
Sweden	Skoal!
Thailand	Chokdee!
The Netherlands	Proost!
	Op uw gezonheid!
Turkey	Serefe!
United States	Cheers!
Wales	Llechyd da! (*yukh-ee daw*)
Yiddish	Mazel tov!

Toasting Notes from Around the World

The Italians are wise before the deed
The Germans in the deed
The French after the deed.
G. Herbert

The German likes his beer
The Pommy likes his half and half
Because it brings good cheer
The Scotsman likes his whisky
And the Irishman likes his hot
The Aussie has no national drink
So he drinks the bloody lot.
Fahey, 1992

In some regions (Central Asia being one), long toasts are preferred. These types of toasts are a form of oration calling for charm and eloquence. Below are some examples.

Presenting *hada*

Present *hada* is a common practice among the Tibetan people to express best wishes on many occasions, such as wedding ceremonies, festivals, visiting the elders and entertaining guests. The white *hada*, a long narrow scarf made of silk, embodies purity and good fortune.

When you come to a Tibetan family, the host will propose a toast, usually barley wine. You should sip three times and then drink up. To entertain guests with tea is a daily etiquette. The guest does not drink until the host has presented the tea.

Add 'la' after saying hello to the Tibetan people to show respect. It is not polite to make any sounds while eating and drinking.

In China

Toasting is a universal way to display respect to those hosting a banquet and to guests. There are several rules.

First, the first person to propose a toast will always be the highest person of authority at the head table hosting the banquet. He/she will rise and express welcome greetings to the group. If the person proposing the toast raises their glass it is customary for everyone seated to also raise the same glass. Once the greeting or toast is given and the toaster has said *ganbei* or taken a drink from his/her own glass, the guests may drink.

Ganbei means 'down the hatch' (literally to drink the entire glass full) so watch the person offering the toast to see if he/she drinks all the contents.

Usually, however, toasts will be a small sip from the glass. The most senior person from the head table will receive the welcome greetings and thank the host for having such a splendid banquet. Later, when timing seems appropriate, the most senior person at the guest's head table will offer a toast to the hosts. Generally toasts can be made at any of the banquet tables, but are always given by the senior person at the table first and always offered first by a host and then followed later by a guest. After official toasts have been completed, everyone is free to toast as desired.

The Chinese do not consume large amounts of alcohol at these functions so it is advisable not to allow drinking/toasting to get out of hand. To get drunk is considered to be a loss of face – or a disgrace to your family, employer and hosts.

Chinese customs

There is a Chinese custom that when married women return to their parents' home or at big festivals (mainly New Product Eating festival and Miao New Year), people 'walk' with a chicken, a bundle of polished glutinous rice, a piece of meat (salt or fresh) and carp. These presents are called 'mixed bundle'. When guests arrive, the host's families not only entertain them, but also call the paternal uncles and cousins and all the members of the village to unwrap the mixed bundle, toast each other in drink and then have dinner. They taste the food brought by the guests to show they are welcoming the guests from far away. This activity is called 'disturbing village' and can last for up to three days.

Proposing toasts is usually done by women. There are two turns: in the first turn, toasts are offered to the host first, and then to the guests; in the second turn, vice versa. Sometimes the oldest one is offered a toast first. Those who are the last to be offered should propose a toast back to express thanks.

Two cups of wine are usually drunk by one person both in the nuptial cup and in proposing toasts. Because people walk with two feet, so they drink two cups of wine. When offering toasts, women hold cups in their hands and sing a toast song loudly:

> *We killed the bull and waited for the coming of honourable guests everyday, but no one came. Today the guests have come to our home by mistake. There is no good wine in jars and no fish and meat in plates. So we can only express our goodwill with pickled cabbage soup.*

The guest takes the cup and continues to sing:

> *I have had the idea to visit relatives for a long time, but I have been busy with family matters and couldn't get free. Today I took the liberty of coming here, and you entertain me warmly. The dishes are full, and nice wine is in jars. I'm very happy and thank my kind host.*

The host and the guest echo each other, and the atmosphere becomes warmer.

In Azerbaijan

A specific person is designated a particular role of toastmaster. In the Azerbaijani language he's called *tamada* (ta-ma-DA), which is derived from two words – *tam* (all, everybody) and *ata* (father), as in *father of all*. It is his responsibility to connect people with each other, guide them, and provide for their well-being.

It's his job to know who all the important guests are, and to introduce them formally by praising them. These speeches are entertaining, informative and spontaneous in nature, and may last up to 10–15 minutes.

Guests expect the *tamada's* performance to be entertaining. If he doesn't do a good job, they'll chat about it and complain. Though there are exceptions to every rule and to every social gathering, a preconceived notion does exist as to what comprises an 'ideal' *tamada* performance!

- Despite being primarily Muslim, most inhabitants of such countries as Uzbekistan do drink alcohol. At a celebration, all the men are given the chance to make a toast, and a long toast is supposed to display intelligence.

- A common Italian wedding toast is *per cent'anni* (for a hundred years) *auguri e figli* (good wishes and male children!). Birthdays: *cento di questi giorni* (a hundred of these days!).

Italians have several toasts for good luck, here are a couple given by Sara Pasin: *in bocca al lupo* (in the mouth of the wolf!). *In culo alla bavena* (your arse to the whale!).

- At a French wedding a toast is made to the newlyweds sometime during the reception. Following the toast, the bride and groom drink from a special double-handled goblet, a *coupe de marriage* that symbolises their new life together. Often they will then pass the goblet to friends and family to share in their joy.

- In Costa Rica *pura vida* (literally, pure life) is used to comment about pretty much anything that is wonderful, including a raised glass.

- In Spain and Latin America, as in many countries, it is appreciated when visitors attempt to give a toast in Spanish. It is also acceptable for women to give toasts.

At weddings and celebrations these are some of the Spanish toasts that can be heard:

- *Arriba*   (glass held high)

- *Abajo*   (glass held low)

- *Al centro*   (glass held out in front)

- *Pa' dentro* or *Adentro*   (drink from glass immediately)

- *Brindamos por ...*   let's drink a toast to ...

4. How to Give a Great Toast

HUUUMM MMM

Over the teeth,
behind the gums,
look out stomach,
here she comes!

In the Moment

The time has come. You are going to give your toast. Depending on the occasion and your role in it, your palms might be a bit wet and your breathing might be shallow.

- Take a few long, deep breaths in and then slowly out expanding your diaphragm. Get out of your head and into the room by looking at the people around you as they eat, drink, and make merry. Feel your body from the feet upwards and focus your energy as you prepare to speak.

- Either stay seated or stand, depending on the size of the group. Get the group's attention gracefully. If seated, ask for their attention; if standing, simply stay silent, glass in hand. Make eye contact with people who look your way – they will catch on and alert their neighbours. Once the group is focused on you and everyone is quiet, start your toast.

- Remember, don't worry about getting it exactly spot on word for word. The reason you practised so much is so that you can be here in the moment and sincerely deliver the sentiment from your heart. If the words change or the phrasing shifts it doesn't matter.

- When you finish (in less than a minute) raise your glass higher and invite everyone to do the same. End with 'cheers!' and stay standing during the response, the glass clinking, and then drink.

- Sit down and move on to enjoying the company and any toasts that follow.

General Guidelines

A toast is a mini speech, and like a speech it is comprised of parts: the opening, the body, and the conclusion. Mini, however, does not mean easy. Any public speaker knows that crafting a good short message is far more difficult than writing a long speech.

Here are some excellent tips for delivering a good toast or short speech. The first is from Winston Churchill:

If you have an important point to make don't try to be subtle or clever.

Use a pile driver. Hit the point once. Then come back and hit it again. Then hit it a third time – a tremendous whack!

Physical preparation tips

Calm your nerves

Visualise yourself as an excellent speaker. Before the event, practise closing your eyes and imagining yourself successfully delivering the toast or short speech in front of the audience. Feel the buzz and excitement of the occasion and allow the fizz to go up from your feet through your body. Use this energy to create a feeling of being centred and present in the room. Practise this on a regular basis before your event.

Breathe deeply from the diaphragm

Do this before you begin and allow this to calm you and help you to feel present with no 'voices' in your head. Before the event practise placing your hands just under your ribcage and feel your ribs move outwards as you breathe in. Let your breath out saying 'woosh' as you do so. Repeat this several times a day until it becomes easy and fluent. After your punchy opening take time to breathe, pause and allow the audience to take in what you have said. This also gives you time to collect your thoughts and take another breath.

Your posture is important

Good posture enables the voice to travel to the outer corners of the room. The vocal cords and breath control are freed up by gently balancing the head on the shoulders. Feel an imaginary thin thread attached to the top of the head pulling up towards the ceiling. Do not force this movement, but keep relaxed with the shoulders down and the arms to your sides. Place your feet equally apart so that you feel stable and in control.

Exercise your vocal cords

Before an event try humming every day. This increases the flexibility of the vocal cords and aids projection.

Eye contact

Remember to keep eye contact with your audience. Pick out several friendly faces to help you to feel relaxed and confident.

Avoid speaking into your drink or down towards the table. Face outwards and smile at the first two rows of people, they are usually very receptive.

Presentation tips

Be brief

In a presentation to the Chicago Literary Club in March 2003, Scott William Petersen asserted that 'a proper toast should be lightly buttered. Neither too much nor too little. Neither too thick or too thin.' This is excellent advice to keep in mind and a good rule of thumb when creating and delivering a toast or mini speech.

When preparing a toast ahead of an event, keep it short and succinct – no more than a minute, and preferably less. The easiest toasts to remember are one or two sentences long. You can write your own, draw from the ones provided here, or do research (there are lots of books and internet sites on the topic, see Resources, pages 134–5) to come up with something appropriate for you and the occasion.

Create a punchy beginning

Start with an unusual quote or surprising fact. If the speech is lasting for longer than the usual toast of under a minute, insert a short story or personal experience to emphasise your point. End on a high and raise your glass with a smile.

Research

Do some research into the background of the person you are toasting or the event at which you are speaking. Use a list or a mind-map to explore ideas and then take no more than three to expand on. Remember that this is about the person you are toasting so make sure it is relevant. Put your main bullet points on a small card if you wish to jog your memory. Avoid using a sheet of paper, as it can be noisy, particularly if you are speaking into a microphone.

Keep it straightforward

Avoid big words unless there is a reason for their inclusion. This is not meant to 'dumb down' your toast. Rather, short and simple words tend to be more forthright and sincere than grand phrasing. Also, try not to repeat yourself or over-use words or phrases.

Focus on the right thing

Remember that you are not the main attraction; rather, you are highlighting some special aspect of the event. Focus on the point of your toast with eloquence and good humour, then close so that people can drink and continue enjoying themselves. Just be yourself, good speakers are not performers.

Do not make potentially offensive jokes

This should go without saying, but must be said anyway. No matter how chummy you are with the toastees, or how informal the occasion, stay tasteful. If you aren't sure if something you want to say is appropriate, don't say it. Alternatively, run it by someone who knows you, the toastees, and the occasion for the toast. If they give you a thumbs down, drop the idea and move on.

Don't read it aloud

Though you should most certainly write out your toast, especially if it is an original piece, when the time comes to deliver it, do not read it. (As mentioned on page 37, use a card with bullet points if you need to.) Ideally rehearse a lot in advance – see the next tip.

Practise, practise, practise

Rehearse the toast or mini speech out loud over and over. Watch yourself in the mirror to make sure your expression and body language work. It is a paradox, but true that rehearsal is needed to sound spontaneous. Do, however, avoid the temptation to memorise it word for word. If you worry about getting it down exactly, you will end up reciting it rather than infusing it with feeling and sincerity. Better to deliver the sentiment accurately even if the words don't end up being precisely the ones you originally wrote down.

On the day

Speak slowly and clearly. It may seem unnatural to you, especially if you tend to talk fast, but slow down your delivery and make a point to enunciate your words. Record yourself while practising so you can hear yourself and get the right speaking speed. Keep practising this speed so that it will come naturally when the actual time comes and your adrenaline is pumping.

Do not deviate from your prepared speech

This may sound opposite to the 'practise, practise, practise' tip, but it targets a different thing. You might experience a burst of inspiration on the spot to add or change your prepared toast. Best not to give in to this temptation. Even with the best of intentions, you could end up saying something you regret. At best, your toast won't be as well delivered if ad-libs are included.

Do not drink too much before you present

Again, this is something that should go without saying. But even with the best of intentions, you may end up drinking more than is wise before delivering your toast. One thing about inebriation, even of the mildest sort, is that we tend to lose our perspective about how 'together' we are ourselves. If the event where you are toasting is particularly convivial – a wedding, for example, or a birthday – you may need to consciously manage your drinking to avoid over consumption of pre-toast alcohol.

Get to know the audience

When you are preparing to give a toast at a large event where you don't know a lot of the attendees, circulate as much as possible before toast time. Connect with people who will be your audience by meeting and greeting. Doing this will help you feel much more comfortable when you stand to propose your toast.

Breathe

Do some deep, slow diaphragmatic breathing before you stand to propose your toast. This will help relax and centre you.

Don't apologise

Don't address your own anxieties and nervousness when you stand up to speak. First of all, attendees may not even notice, so why draw attention? Second, this puts the spotlight on you rather than the attendees which, as noted previously, isn't the right focus.

Keep in mind that you have a sympathetic audience

Attendees aren't sitting there waiting for you to fail. They want to enjoy your toast and join you in celebrating the toastees. So don't worry if you stumble over a word or forget a line; your audience will still love you.

DIY Toasts

If your work or personal life style is 'toast-full', and you are routinely in a position to lead a glass raising, you might consider committing a few short toasts to memory. I have included a collection of simple toasts in this book to give you some material to pull from. Whether you use the toasts included here or use words that you find elsewhere, understand the source and context of any toasts or quotes that you make your own, and match the piece to the occasion. It's best to assume that your listeners will look up your source, so use quotes that work in their original setting. You don't want to pull the one complimentary line from a poem that is actually negative and critical.

You may prefer, or the event may require, penning your own 'mini speech'. If so, keep these points in mind.

- Open with words complimenting what has just gone before, or anticipating what's coming next. Alternatively, make a favourable remark about the group in general.

- Proceed to the body of the toast by developing your theme. Stay light, be witty, keep it short. Humour is great if the occasion permits and if the humour will be appreciated by everyone, not just a chosen few (see the next chapter for more about humour).

- Conclude with a graceful compliment to the person or group you are toasting. End on a positive note and clearly indicate that the time has come for the response and the clink by raising your glass or using some other accepted gesture.

- Above all relax and enjoy it – if you do the audience will too.

> **To public speaking:**
> You'd scarce expect one of my age
> To speak in public on the stage
> And if I chance to fall below
> Demosthenes or Cicero
> Don't view me with a critic's eye,
> But pass my imperfections by.
> Large streams from little fountains flow
> Tall oaks from little acorns grow.
> David Everett

5. Roasting Toasting

I drink to your charm,
your beauty and your brains,
which gives you a rough idea
how hard up I am for a drink.
Groucho Marx

Nothing says 'we love you!' like poking fun at someone. The closer our relationship to the target of our words, in fact, the more likely we are to tease and joke, and the more likely the target will appreciate it and be amused. After a laugh people are more receptive to the message that immediately follows it. It follows logically, then, that many toasting occasions lend themselves well to humour.

The use of humour in any public speech is a delicate matter. What is funny to one person or group of people might be puzzling or downright insulting to another.

Toasting and Humour: What Not to Do

Keep these warnings in mind when using humour in a toast.

- **The funny stuff needs to fit the event**. Some toasting opportunities are part of significant life milestones, while others are lighter in tone. If you want to use humour in your toast, make sure you respect the nature of the occasion.

- **Keep it clean in public**. Save your store of bawdy toasts for intimate evenings with your closest friends. When toasting in any other group, keep the humour fit for general consumption.

- **Ethnic or demographic humour**. Avoid jokes that focus on a particular nationality, ethnic origin, geographic location, or other demographic category.

- **Don't leave people out**. Don't tell stories or jokes that only a few people will understand.

Getting the Humour Right

If these warnings have stopped you in your tracks, take heart. Even if you can't come up with something original, funny, and appropriate to the occasion, you can still add humour to your toast.

When in doubt, the best way to add laughter to your toast is through quotations. Using funny words of a famous person will help in two ways. First, you can have confidence that the words actually are funny – they wouldn't be cited otherwise. Second, you personally have some distance from the quote. If by some chance the quote falls flat, the only thing you can be criticised for is your ability to choose wisely, which is far better than leaving people with the impression that you are boring.

It is relatively easy to find quotations. First, there are any number of compilations in book form, available at a bookstore or library. There are also a large number of sites on the internet that list quotations for all kind of subjects. One good site is www.thinkexist.com. Membership (which is required after a first few pages of search results) is free, and includes the ability to store and tag quotations that you like.

If you do your research and come up with a great quote that fits the occasion exactly, but that is attributed to someone who is not likely to be recognisable to your audience, don't despair. Instead of saying, 'as Thucydides wrote', say 'as an ancient Greek historian once wrote', or 'a wise old Greek said ...'

If you want to use a quotation, or even just a few words of a well-known quotation, make sure you check out its context. It can be a real laughter killer to use a quote that is funny out of context, but that was actually said or written in a completely different vein.

Using cartoons

If you still feel that introducing humour is a challenge for you then try this. Tell a cartoon – yes, I really meant tell it. Verbally describe a cartoon and link it to the point you are trying to make. Cartoons make great speech material because they are so varied. Check out your local newspapers and visit the free websites that provide a wealth of cartoons to choose from; www. cartoonbank.com is just one example.

So how do you tell a cartoon? Let's imagine you are a manager of a small business that has just completed a very successful year, but the senior staff have not had time to sit down and really take stock, as they have been so busy. You could begin the celebration by saying:

I saw a cartoon yesterday by Matthew Diffee, where a family of six were sitting down at the dining room table and the father said 'before we begin this family meeting, how about we go around and say our names and a little something about ourselves?'.

Well, I believe we know each others' names, but right now I am feeling a little like that father ...

Or perhaps you are celebrating your sixtieth birthday. You could start your thank you speech with this little cartoon by Leo Cullum:

'I have rolled my pension over and over and over, and now I have no idea where the hell it is.'

Luckily our financial advisor managed to locate it for me and we are now able to celebrate my birthday with part of it – cheers!

Always make sure that the cartoon is related to the occasion you are celebrating and pause before and after the punchline to create tension and to give people time to grasp the meaning. Remember that you have practised it, but this is the first time they will be hearing it.

Finding jokes from your life

Humour does not mean the kind of jokes that get rolling belly laughs, mild humour is fine and the best humour comes from your own life. Jokes told on the internet are old hat by the time you tell them and using amusing snap-shots of your own life or those of friends and family are always well received. If you know you are going to be called on to give a short speech or to propose a toast, keep a notebook of amusing remarks you hear at work and around the home. You will be surprised at how many you will collect if you pay attention to them and note them all down. Pay attention to the context too, as it is easy to forget why the incident was funny at the time.

What if they don't laugh?

So what happens if they don't laugh? Above all don't panic and don't show it on your face. Pretend that you didn't mean to be funny at all and just continue as before. Any kind of public speaking is a learning curve. Take this away and learn from it.

A doctor friend of mine whose name is John Postlethwaite told me this little story:

I was once introduced before making a toast by a nervous master of ceremonies who said, instead of 'pray silence for'…, 'pray for silence from Mr Postlethwaite! Needless to say people found this great fun and my speech got off to a good start.

Funny Quotations for a Raised Glass

Following are quotations and toasts that you can use when you want to add laughter to the occasion without risk.

It is better to have loafed and lost, than never to have loafed at all.
James Thurber

There is a theory which states that if ever for any reason anyone discovers what exactly the universe is for and why it is here it will instantly disappear and be replaced by something even more bizarre and inexplicable. There is another that states that this has already happened.
Douglas Adams

A good wife and health is a man's best wealth.
T. Fuller

You live and learn. At any rate, you live.
Douglas Adams

Safe Humorous Toasts and Quotes

As you slide down the banister of life,
may the splinters never point the wrong way.

Accept that some days you're the pigeon, and some days you're the statue.

Here's to the English summer
Three hot days and a thunderstorm.
19th century

To friends – who are like fiddle strings
They must not be screwed too tight.
H.G. Bohn

To the men I've loved,
To the men I've kissed,
My heartfelt apologies
To the men I've missed!

Lift them high, and drain them dry!
To the one who says, 'my turn to buy!'

Laugh and the world laughs with you.
Weep and it laughs at you.

May we never lose our bait when we fish for compliments.

Here's to the hair of the dog that bit you.
J. Haywood

To life – it is half spent before we know what it is.
G.H. Bohn

Love and scandal are the best sweeteners of tea.
Henry Fielding

To a man not old, but mellow, like good wine.
Stephen Phillips

Oh don't the days seem lank and long
When all goes right and nothing goes wrong
And isn't your life extremely flat
With nothing whatever to grumble at!
Sir William Gilbert Schwenck

Here's to age and remember…
It is better to wear out than rust out.
Richard Cumberland

———

Some Guinness was spilt on the barroom floor
When the pub was shut for the night.
When out of his hole crept a wee brown mouse
And stood in the pale moonlight.
He lapped up the frothy foam from the floor
Then back on his haunches he sat.
And all night long, you could hear the mouse roar,
'Bring on the goddamn cat!'
Irish

———

An Irish story that may not be quite as safe for every audience

John O'Reilly hoisted his beer and said, 'Here's to spending the rest of me life between the legs of me wife!' That won him the top prize at the pub for the best toast of the night!

He went home and told his wife, Mary, 'I won the prize for the best toast of the night.' She said, 'aye, did ye now? And what was your toast?' John said, 'Here's to spending the rest of me life sitting in church beside me wife.' 'Oh, that is very nice indeed, John!' Mary said.

The next day, Mary ran into one of John's drinking buddies on the street corner. The man chuckled leeringly and said, 'John won the prize the other night at the pub with a toast about you, Mary.'

She said, 'aye, he told me, and I was a bit surprised myself. You know he's only been there twice in the last four years.

Once he fell asleep, and the other time I had to pull him by the ears to make him come.'

6. Wedding Toasting

You're not going to believe the wedding we went to last week. The best man started his toast with 'I've got a confession to make ...'
Brad Paisley

Of all the social occasions where toasting occurs, the wedding is by far the most common. Other types of social events may come and go without any toasts being proposed, but a wedding without a toast is rare indeed.

Useful Facts That Can Be Woven Into Wedding Toasts and Speeches

Honeymoon

In many societies the consummation of the marriage is more important than the ceremony itself – to the family as well as to the bride and groom. The term honeymoon was used for when consummation takes place. It derives from an old Northern European custom of drinking honeyed wine or mead as an aphrodisiac during the first month of marriage.

It was once customary among the peasants of Languedoc in France for friends to burst into the bridal chamber and offer the newlyweds soup from a chamber pot. The soup was meant to endow the couple with vigour, so ensuring that their marriage would be quickly blessed with children.

Newly married couples of seventeenth-century Brittany were expected to wait three nights before consummating their marriage. The first night was dedicated to God, the second to St Joseph and the third to the groom's personal patron saint.

The veil

Many of the present-day wedding customs that we take for granted are really born of age-old traditions. The wedding veil was introduced by ancient Greeks and Romans to protect the bride from the evil eye of a jealous rival suitor.

The wedding ring

The wedding ring dates back to the ancient Egyptians. The ring is placed on the third finger of the bride's hand because this was the finger that carried the vein that led directly to the heart. The ring made of gold, the most enduring of metals, signifies a perfect and life-long union.

The trousseau derived from the old French *trousse*, or small bundle of valuables that was originally paid to the husband. Until a century ago in most parts of the Balkans, the bride was expected to provide her groom with sets of underwear which she had made herself.

Throwing rice or confetti

This custom at weddings has its origins in an old Greek fertility rite of showering sweetmeat over the couple and was meant to confer prosperity on them.

The wedding cake

Giving out pieces of cake originated in a Roman custom of breaking bread over the head of the bride for prosperity. Each guest then took away a portion of the bread for luck.

True Wedding Toast Stories, or What Not to Do

There are many wedding toasts from hell out there. The following are great examples of how *not* to toast the bride and groom.

Here's one from the father of the bride:

I've seen my daughter grow through the years and have had a few laughs, like the time she fell in the toilet as a small child. She was so mad at me for laughing at her, that I think maybe that's why it took her so long to find a man to marry.

And yet another from a father giving his daughter away in marriage:

Well, this isn't what I would have wanted for you, but I guess it's too late now.

A mother of a groom toasted her son with:

You come from a long line of broken marriages, so don't break the trend!

A best man stood up at one wedding and started off with:

Life is a bitch. You never know where you are going to be. You never know what the future will bring. You might be happy, or you might be divorced in a year.

(Interestingly, the bride and groom *were* divorced within a year. Maybe he had some method to his madness!)

Besides wedding toasts that aren't appropriate to the occasion, there are those that go on and on. Stories of best man toasts that ramble along for ten, fifteen, or more minutes while everyone sits numbly by are common among wedding goers.

Wedding Toasts at the Main Table

Whether a small family affair or an enormous sit-down reception, there is a common protocol for toasting the newlyweds. At a wedding reception at which a meal is served, toasts are offered once all of the guests have been seated and have been served their drinks. At less formal wedding receptions, toasts should be offered after everyone has gone through the receiving line and has been served a drink.

At English wedding receptions the first toast is proposed by the bride's father, or, if he is not present for some reason, an older male relative (perhaps the person who gave the bride away during the wedding ceremony).

The Father of the Bride

A toast to give if you are the father of the bride

My greatest wish for the two of you is that through the years your love for each other will so deepen and grow that years from now you will look back on this day, your wedding day, as the day you loved each other the least.
Simran Khurana

Guidelines for the father of the bride/partner

Wise words from a father of the bride on two occasions – John Postlethwaite:

I was terrified by the thought of having to stand up in front of all my friends and colleagues and give a speech. I am not someone who generally pushes himself forward and this was a daunting task. However, after my first attempt I realised that at a wedding most people are determined to enjoy themselves and are usually very merry by the time of the speeches. You only have to stand up and everyone laughs.

These are my top tips for the father of the bride:

1. Every time you pause everyone is highly amused and seeing double entendres that aren't there. So the way to go about it is to take your time and smile and everyone smiles with you.

2. Start by 'talking up' the occasion as the audience have taken a lot of trouble to be there and want to feel good.

3. Thank everyone profusely for coming to this wonderfully happy occasion etc … and single out people by name for a special mention.

4. Mention the grandparents, people who have come a long way and those from abroad if relevant.

5. Make a joke about them having to negotiate the traffic on the M25 or a particular black spot near you – congratulate them on their safe arrival.

6. Make people smile by thanking your wife (or whoever managed the event) and weave in a special comment if there were any fraught or amusing moments.

7. Suggest that people come to you if they have any complaints about the car parking, lack of wine or a drunken relation!

8. Turn to the groom and let him know that this is how things will be from now on – all complaints will come to him and praise to the wife!

9. If you need to mention absent/departed friends or relations do so at the beginning of your speech and try to bring in a kind or amusing comment about their life or personality. Make sure you keep it brief.

10. One amusing way to start is to say that, in the interests of spontaneity, you have made a pact with the groom to use absolutely no notes. Then after a pause pull out a large pad of notes while turning to the groom and saying 'you didn't believe me, did you?' (Best to arrange with the groom in advance and then he can pull out his notes and wave them at you.)

11. By all means use notes but try your best not to read them. People need time to absorb your words so go very slowly and keep eye contact. Remember alcohol dulls the intellect as well as tickling the chuckle muscle.

12. Of course profusely compliment the bride. Use adjectives such as beautiful, stunning, talented, amazing, etc. And each often gets a cheer if you say them slowly enough.

13. Pick out positive aspects of the bride's life and allow time for her friends and relations to nod in agreement and give a cheer. I mentioned that my daughter had been lucky in love (I nodded towards the groom and all his friends cheered!).

14. Develop a theme around some of the more successful and amusing elements of your daughter's life – relate them to a hobby or pastime.

15. Give a bit of life history emphasising achievements and successes and telling a few amusing anecdotes. Use photos of past exploits if you have them.

16. If there are any cheers or clapping allow the noise to die down before proceeding as it is difficult to speak against your audience and you want to be heard. They will eventually stop.

17. Speak twice as loudly and slowly as you normally do – only you know what you are about to say and your audience needs time to take in your jokes and stories.

18. Never tell a story that may compromise or embarrass anyone present as this can have on-going repercussions and may fall terribly flat.

19. Keep it short and finish by once again praising, complimenting and thanking the audience – they love it!

20. Then thank your daughter with a special comment or quote.

The Groom

The groom's speech

His/her speech should include thanks to the father-in-law for his toast, the bride's parents, his/her own parents, and the guests. Thank the guests and family for any gifts received. He/she should compliment his/her new wife/partner, thank the best man/woman and other helpers, and express regrets for absent family members or friends. He/she then proposes a toast to the bridesmaids/pageboys. He/she may elect to present gifts to the attendants at this point.

Guidelines for the groom's speech

• Open by welcoming friends and/or family.

• Thank them for coming and for supporting you.

• Thank the bride's parents/parent for helping to make this day special for you and your wife/partner.

- Say something complimentary about the day so far and the organisers.

- Now turn to your new wife/partner and offer thanks for some of his/her best qualities (why you asked her/him to be your wife/partner!).

- Let your partner/wife know what you hope to have in your future married life together (both positive and amusing/witty comments).

- Make the speech amusing if you can by bringing in some incidents from your lives together so far (where you met, how you first spoke, what first attracted you).

- Use an appropriate quote from the book.

- Raise your glass and invite others to do the same.

- Make a toast to the future, to your wife/partner and what you hope will be in your future life together.

The Best Man/Woman

Guidelines for the best man's/woman's speech

- Thank the guests for their patience when listening to the speeches.

- Say a few words of thanks for the friendship that you have had with the groom.

- Say a little about the stag party if you had one.

- Comment favourably on the outfits/dresses and décor in the hall or church.

- Find one or two interesting/amusing things/incidents that have happened/changed since your friend met his/her future partner.

• If this is a second marriage – mention why, in your opinion, this one will last!

• Tell a couple of interesting stories from the past about your friend that others may not know. (Don't embarrass your friend too much, this is his/her big day not yours!)

• Mention the absent family members or friends.

• Read out the messages or cards from those who cannot attend.

• Thank the bridesmaids, attendants, musicians and catering staff (if the wedding was prepared by the family – thank them).

• Hand over to the Toastmaster (if you have one) or announce the cutting of the cake.

• Raise your glass in a toast to the bride and groom/partners (see suitable toasts in the book).

Other Toasts

Gay weddings and partnerships

Obviously not all weddings are traditional and the gay marriage will create traditions and customs over the coming years. Most of the toasts are appropriate for all marriages and partnerships, but there are a few gay marriage toasts added at the end of this section.

A toast to the bridesmaids

> *We admire them for their beauty, respect them for their intelligence, adore them for their virtues, and love them because we can't help it.*
> Simran Khurana

The best man/woman then replies on behalf of the bridesmaids and proposes a toast of his/her own.

Toast:

> *Thank you for your kind words. We have not done great things, but we have done small things today with great love. I seem to remember that great things happen when you do the small things right! Cheers.*
> Author's adaptation from a quote by Mother Teresa

American wedding toast protocol is slightly different, though the tone and intent remain the same. The order for the raising of glasses is:

- best man

- fathers (first the groom's, then the bride's)

- groom

- bride

- friends and relatives

- maid/matron of honour

- mothers (first the groom's, then the bride's).

If you are giving a toast as one of the 'featured players' at a wedding – parent of bride or groom, maid of honour, or best man – no one will be surprised if your toast takes a few minutes. But 'a few' means three or four, at most five, minutes. Follow the mini-speech format, keep your reminiscences favourable to both bride and groom, and end with an eloquent wish for a bright future together.

Toasts from the rest of the guests

After the 'main players' have spoken, other guests may wish to say a few words and propose their own toasts. The best man/woman or Toastmaster should know beforehand if there will be any additional speeches so that they can oversee the proceedings.

If you are a guest and wish to propose a toast to the bride and groom, keep it very short, like the examples that follow. Save your anecdotes and long expressions of well wishing for the video camera operator (if there is one) or a one-on-one chat with the bride and/or groom.

Let people know your relationship to the bride and/or groom as part of your toast. Keep the significance of the event in mind. Do not make references to the honeymoon, any previous marriages or liaisons, future family, or sex. And don't end up giving a nightmare toast by including something negative like, 'and I hope theirs doesn't end in divorce like mine did'.

Some Simple Wedding Toasts

Here are some simple lines that can stand alone or be added to your own personal wish for the newlyweds.

As your wedding ring wears – your cares will wear away.
J. Ray

A good wife and health is a man's best wealth.
(T. Fuller)

May 'for better or worse' be far better than worse!

A toast to love and laughter and happiness ever after!

May all your hopes and dreams come true,
and may the memory of this day
become more dear with each passing year.

May the roof above you never fall in and may you both never fall out.

(The above are taken from cards and have not been accredited.) A couple of humorous wedding toasts taken from proverbs:

It is a good horse that never stumbles
And a good wife that never grumbles.
J. Ray

To the lamp of love – may it burn brightest in the darkest hours and never flicker in the winds of trial.
Simran Khurana

Keep your eyes wide open before marriage
And half shut afterwards.
B. Franklin

And remember:

The way to an Englishman's heart is through his stomach.
Nineteenth century

The wife is the key of the house.
T. Draxe

Marriage is like a stone
It would be too smooth if it had no rubs in it.
T. Fuller

Marriage: A community consisting of a master, a mistress, and two slaves
– making in all, two.
Simran Khurana

A toast from groom to bride:

> *To my wife – But what is woman?*
> *Only one of nature's agreeable blunders.*
> Hannah Cowley

> *To my wife – she would be (even) more charming if one could*
> *fall into her arms without falling into her hands.*
> Ambrose Bierce

A toast from bride to groom:

> *Never love unless you can*
> *Bear with all the fruits of man:*
> *Men will sometimes jealous be,*
> *Though but little cause they see.*
> Thomas Campion

Gay Wedding Toasts

> *To you –*
> *I found you down in Brighton beside the pale blue sea*
> *You asked me if I'd marry and I said – 'that's not for me'*
> *But you took me to the local bars and oh, to Gay Pride too*
> *Now I'm glad I came down south and yes, I'll say 'I do!'*

> *To the happy pair:*
> *May your luck spread like jam*
> *May it be the best year yet for you*
> *May you all look back happily on this day*
> *May you find peace in everything you do.*

> *Proud to be gay, it is your right*
> *Step out boldly and embrace tonight.*

7. Sample Toasts – An A–Z

Toasts should be like a woman's skirt – short enough to be interesting, yet long enough to cover the subject.
Mary Mitchell

When it comes to toasting, the challenge for most of us is not the grand dinner or celebrity gala. It is usually the need to come up with words to grace a birthday, anniversary, wedding, or some other gathering of family and friends.

With the huge resource that the internet provides finding the right toast for whatever occasion you encounter should be fairly easy. This section therefore lists the most obvious occasions for toasting and what kind of toasts or quotes would be appropriate. Some standard toasts are provided for each occasion to give you a quick and easy reference.

Standard toasts, whether in this book or in another resource, will come in various types. Some are direct quotes from written works, as in:

May you be merry and lack nothing.
William Shakespeare

Others are couched in the flowery language of previous generations, such as:

Then here's to thee, old friend; and long
May thou and I thus meet,
To brighten still with wine and song
This short life ere it fleet.

You may never encounter a situation where this kind of expression fits. Most toasts you will hear and propose will be short, modern, and to the point. The examples listed here, therefore, will be in today's tongue where possible.

Accomplishment Toasts/Quotes

When people accomplish something together it is always an occasion for a toast and a celebratory drink. The accomplishment can be a family affair or the celebration of a successful business deal, a promotion, a team success or an individual sporting event.

Here are some sample toasts and quotes to celebrate these occasions.

To your attitude!
It is not your aptitude, but your <u>attitude</u>, that determines your altitude.
Zig Ziglar

It's how you deal with failure that determines how you achieve success.
David Feherty

Here's to…

Optimism, it is the one quality more associated with success and happiness than any other.
Brian Tracey

In the confrontation between the stream and the rock, the stream always wins, not through strength but by perseverance.
H. Jackson Brown

I get up, I walk, I fall down. Meanwhile I keep dancing.
Renee Locks

To your success – you took the challenge to be yourself In a world that is trying to make you like everyone else.
Renee Locks

Age

Old age is like climbing a mountain. You climb from ledge to ledge and the higher you get the more tired and breathless you become, but your views become more extensive.
Ingrid Bergman

He who is of a calm and happy nature will hardly feel the pressure of age But to him who is of an opposite disposition, youth and age are equally a burden.
Plato

All-Occasion

May our glasses always be full and our hearts follow suit.

Here's to turkey when you're hungry,
champagne when you're dry,
a lover when you need one,
and heaven when you die.

May the single all be married
and the married all be happy.
Love to one, friendship to many, and good-will to all.

The only way to keep your health is to eat what you don't
want, drink what you don't like, and do what you'd rather not.
Mark Twain

May you have warm words on a cold evening, a full moon on a
dark night, and a smooth road all the way to your door.

To lying, cheating, stealing, and drinking:
May you lie to save your brother,
may you cheat death,
may you steal a woman's heart and may you drink with me.

May you always work like you don't need money,
dance like there's nobody watching,
and love like it's never going to hurt.

May you have the hindsight to know where you've been;
the foresight to know where you are going;
and the insight to know when you've gone too far.

Anniversary

Anniversary toasts can cover as much ground as birthday toasts. Celebrating the first year of marriage can cause glasses to be raised, as can celebrating the seventy-fifth year. And like birthdays, your relationship to the celebrants will be as much a factor in coming up with the right toast as the year being toasted to.

Here are some toasts and quotes to apply to any wedding anniversaries that call for a glass to be raised.

May the warmth of your affection melt the frosts of old age.

Anniversaries come and anniversaries go –
but may your happiness together go on forever.

Love seems the swiftest, but it is the slowest of all growths. No man or woman really knows what perfect love is until they have been married a quarter of a century.
Mark Twain

Marriage is a wonderful institution … but who wants to live in an institution?
Groucho Marx

Keep your eyes wide open before marriage, and half-shut afterwards.
Benjamin Franklin

Marriage is three parts love and seven parts forgiveness of sins.
Lao Tzu, founder of Taoism

There is no more lovely, friendly, and charming relationship, communion, or company than a good marriage.
Martin Luther

*A successful marriage requires falling in love many times,
always with the same person.*
Mignon McLaughlin, American journalist

*This is what marriage really means: helping one another
to reach the full status of being persons, responsible beings
who do not run away from life.*
Paul Tournier, Swiss physician

Birthday

In the world of toasts, those given on birthdays have to be most varied. This is certainly not a 'one size fits all' category. A birthday can be a cause for honest celebration or it can be an occasion for sympathy, either real or (usually) humorous. It can be a time to honour a great friendship, or it can be a more formal salute to a boss or co-worker.

Here is a general, all-occasion birthday toast that can stand alone or conclude a more personal sentiment:

> *Here's to your birthday [name],
> and may God bless you with many more!*

Here are examples of general toasts that tend towards the humorous-sympathy side:

*You're not as young as you used to be,
but you're not as old as you're going to be!*

*Another candle on your cake? Well there's no cause to pout.
Just be glad that you have the strength to blow the damn thing
out!*

To you on your birthday, with glass held high
Glad you're the one that's older, not I!

We know we're getting old when the only thing
we want for our birthday is not to be reminded of it.

A true friend remembers your birthday but not your age.

Birthdays are nature's way of telling us to eat more cake.

May you live as long as you want and never want as long as
you live.

Health, wealth and happiness – and the time to enjoy them.

Birthdays – special:

Besides the 'regular' birthdays, there are the milestone birthdays – ages twenty-one, thirty, forty, fifty and beyond. And there are birthdays of specific people in our lives – wife, husband, child, parents, in-laws and siblings. Then there are mixtures of the two – a child's twenty-first, for example, or a mother-in-law's eightieth.

Toasts to family members on special birthdays are made special when you include a memory from the past. If you can include a visual aid in the form of a photograph, so much the better. Humour is always good; a funny story delivered before raising your glass to the person celebrating their birthday will be appreciated by everyone. Just make sure the story isn't overly embarrassing!

If you need to compose a toast to celebrate a milestone birthday for someone you don't know well, one great strategy is to do a bit of research about the day in question. What was the news of the day when the celebrant came into the world? Who were the biggest film celebrities? What books were being read and talked about?

Sharing two or three of the best titbits as part of your toast will make your contribution memorable.

Here are some quotations that can be used for milestone birthday toasts:

Birthdays are feathers in the broad wing of time.
Jean Paul Richter, German novelist

Most of us can remember a time when a birthday – especially if it was one's own – brightened the world as if a second sun has risen.
Robert Lynd, Irish essayist

To staying young – live honestly, eat slowly, and lie about your age.
Lucille Ball

I never know what to get my father for his birthday. I gave him some money and said, 'Buy yourself something that will make your life easier.' So he went out and bought a present for my mother.
Rita Rudner, American comedienne

Maturity has more to do with what types of experiences you've had, and what you've learned from them, and less to do with how many birthdays you've celebrated.

Beautiful young people are accidents of nature, but beautiful old people are works of art.
Eleanor Roosevelt

Business Toasts and Short Speeches

An introduction to a workshop or presentation by a guest speaker

It is a good idea to ask the speaker to provide you with a brief bio and a particular piece of information that may surprise the audience. This could be an unusual fact, a surprising statistic or an unusual hobby or pastime.

I'd now like to introduce (name) as you know he/she is …
(a little information on the person and his/her topic plus the surprise fact or unusual story).
Please would you give a warm welcome to (repeat name).

At the end of a session by a guest speaker/invited guest

I would like to thank (name) on behalf of everyone present and we particularly enjoyed (try to find a special moment/element you liked).
Once again many thanks to (name) (you lead the applause).

On the final day or successful completion of a particular project

We would like to thank you for your excellent contribution to the success of this product/service … it's …

Not the toil but the chase
Not the project but the race
Not the hours but the play
Plus the bonus paid today!
Cheers and thanks to you all.

Thanking your team/colleagues

I would like to take this opportunity to thank all the staff for their efforts over the (past year/six months etc) and to propose a toast to you all on your excellent achievements – Cheers!

Representing a group or your company

On behalf of (company name) I would like to say a few words of thanks/appreciation for your (generous hospitality/interesting presentation, etc) and to raise a toast to a (successful future partnership, the next time we meet, etc)

Business celebrations of all kinds

*On this special day fill up the glass
So it glistens on the brink
Be it red wine, white wine, port or beer
Let's celebrate and drink!*
Jackie Arnold

*A bottle of good wine, like a good act
Shines ever in the retrospect.*
Robert Louis Stevenson

Welcome and introductions to business meetings

Welcome everyone. I/We would like to start by (your introduction). Then we will move on to (your main points/theme) and conclude by (summary of what went before).

It is always useful to start with a quote. Here's an example before a sales meeting.

I would like to start with a toast from Bill Copeland: 'Here's to becoming top banana, without losing sight of the bunch.'

Welcome to visitors (often from overseas)

Here we speak English, drink milk with our tea
You're welcome to join us, not far from the sea
Eat porridge for breakfast, marmite on toast
The best Yorkshire pudding on Sunday with roast
Beer with a head on it, port with the cheese
Just be at home here, some wine if you please.
Cheers!
Jackie Arnold

Farewell speech when resigning

When saying farewell you are closing a period, a career, or a position you have held and giving your reasons for leaving. It could also describe your emotions and feelings towards the people, your position and/or the place you are leaving.

A few tips to get you started. Include:

• something positive about the situation and why you are leaving.

• your feelings and emotions (hopefully positive).

• a little about your future plans (if appropriate).

• thanks.

For a toast to end on here is an example:

I've made mistakes but I'll learn from them
I'll meet them head on and not turn from them
I'll take the knowledge and build on it
Toast my departure? Depend on it!
Jackie Arnold

If you are toasting the one leaving:

- Thank the person for their loyalty/hard work/personality.

- Find something special or unusual they contributed.

- Tell a short story about an event/idea/action they were involved in.

- Wish them luck in the future (if you know where/why they are going mention this – with their permission).

- Present them with a small gift if appropriate. A toast to send them on their way:

> *An employee with an active mind*
> *Someone who's helpful and generally kind*
> *A person who always is able to think*
> *That's the one I'd invite for a drink!*
> *Cheers.*

Christening

Christenings are not as common these days as many parents believe that children should choose their own beliefs when they are older. But families often gather to celebrate the new arrival and below are some useful quotes to bring a smile to the faces of the new parents.

> *If I had influence with the good fairy who is supposed to preside over the christening of all children, I should ask that her gift to each child in the world be a sense of wonder so indestructible that it would last throughout life.*
> Rachel Carson

A toast to you on this day of your birth:
'Be yourself, believe in yourself and stand tall in a world that
often prefers to mould you to the mind and shape of everyone
else.'
Jackie Arnold

Raise your glasses please
We'll celebrate till dawn
Champagne corks pop, dance till you drop
My son/daughter's just been born.
Jackie Arnold

May the awareness and curiosity about everything around you
today stay with you for the rest of your life.
Jackie Arnold

Do you know what it is to be a child?
It is to believe in love, to believe in loveliness, to believe in belief,
It is to be so little that the elves can reach to whisper in your ear,
It is to turn pumpkins into coaches, and mice into horses,
lows into highs and nothing into everything,
For each child has its fairy godmother in its own soul.
Francis Thomas

Christmas

To Christmas … It comes but once a year.
But when it comes it brings good cheer.

Heap on more wood – the wind is chill
But let it whistle as it will
We'll keep our Christmas merry still.
Sir Walter Scott

May all your Christmas dreams come true
May family be around
May all the trees be white with snow
As you hear the laughter sound.

Christmas – oh what shall we do!
Who shall we invite?
Let's take off to sunny skies
Let's pack and go tonight!
Cheers!

To wish you peace and happiness
Today and all next year
May love surround you, warm your heart
And fill you with good cheer.

To all the twinkle in the stars tonight
To all the snowflakes falling
To all those candles burning bright
To all those children calling.

Confidence

Whether you think you can or think you can't, you're right.
Henry Ford

You have to expect things of yourself before you can do them.
Michael Jordan

You are educated when you have the ability to listen to almost anything without losing your temper or self-confidence.
Robert Frost

Courage

Life is mostly froth and bubble, Two things stand like stone –
Kindness in another's trouble, Courage in your own.
Adam L. Gordon

Man cannot discover new oceans unless he has the courage to
lose sight of the shore.
André Gide

Love is the most difficult and dangerous form of courage.
Courage is the most desperate, admirable and noble kind
of love.
Delmore Schwartz

The only service a friend can really render is to keep up your
courage by holding up to you a mirror in which you can see a
noble image of yourself.
George Bernard Shaw

Life is a series of experiences, each one of which makes us
bigger, even though it is hard to realise this. For the world was
built to develop character, and we must learn that the setbacks
and grieves which we endure help us in our marching onward.
Henry Ford

To love someone deeply gives you strength. Being loved by
someone deeply gives you courage.
Lao Tzu (sixth century B.C.), legendary Chinese
philosopher

Friendship

Sometimes friends will leave to find a new job or to move abroad.
Here are some useful toasts and quotes if they do.

May our friend in sorrow never be a sorrowing friend.

There is no one alive who is Youer than you.
Dr. Seuss

May the hinges of friendship never grow rusty.

*To friends: may we always have them
and always know their value.*

*To friends: may we never lack one to cheer us,
or a home to welcome them.*

*May we never have friends who, like shadows,
keep close to us in the sunshine
only to desert us in a cloudy day or in the night.*

*He has a capacity for enjoyment so vast
that he gives away great chunks to those about him,
and never even misses them.*
Dorothy Parker

*There are not many things in life so beautiful as true
friendship, and not many things more uncommon.*

True friendship is seen through the heart, not through the eyes.

*A friendship founded on business is better
than a business founded on friendship.*

Good company, good wine, good welcome make good people.
Shakespeare

And finally!

> *Here's to you and here's to me,*
> *Friends may we always be!*
> *But, if by chance we disagree,*
> *Up yours! Here's to me!*

Funerals

Toasting to a dearly departed friend or family member is not always part of the funeral ritual. It depends on cultural traditions and how things are arranged after the service. If the post-funeral arrangement is more of an open house, with people coming and going over a period of time, it is unlikely that there will be a group toasting session. If this gathering is more in the order of a wake, with the group in attendance and together for several hours, there will probably be some toasts proposed.

Even if no toasts are offered right after the loss of someone in your family or social circle, there will certainly be occasions other than the day of the funeral to raise a glass in memory. If you are inspired to honour someone's memory, here are some short but eloquent toasts.

To live in hearts we leave behind is not to die.

A little while with grief and laughter,
And then the day will close
The shadows gather ... what comes after
No man knows.

Here's to other meetings
and merry meetings then
and here's to those we've drunk with
and never can again.

Every mortal loss is an immortal gain.
William Blake

No one's death comes to pass without making some
impression, and those close to the deceased inherit part of the
liberated soul and become richer in their humaneness.
Hermann Broch

We sometimes congratulate ourselves at the moment of
waking from a troubled dream; it may be so the moment
after death.
Nathaniel Hawthorne

His life was gentle; and the elements
so mixed in him, that Nature might stand up,
and say to all the world, THIS WAS A MAN!
William Shakespeare

Remember me when I am gone away
Gone far away into the silent land...
But if you should forget me for a while
And afterwards remember, do not grieve.
Better by far that you should forget and smile
Than that you should remember and be sad.
Christina Rossetti

All the world's a stage,
And all the men and women merely players;
They have their exits and their entrances;
And one man in his time plays many parts.
William Shakespeare

Health

Health to our bodies, peace to our minds
And plenty to our boards.
Eighteenth century

The best doctors in the world are Doctor Diet,
Doctor Quiet and Dr Merryman.
Jonathan Swift

Here's to your very excellent health
Eat moderately well and drink wine
A good strong heart for the rest of your life
Lets drink to them both, yours and mine!

Life

Cool breeze
Warm fire
Full moon
Easy chair
Empty plates
Soft words
Sweet songs
Tall tales
Short sips
Long life
John Egerton

Happiness is not so much in having as sharing. We make a
living by what we get, but we make a life by what we give.
Norman Macewan

Be not afraid of life. Believe that life is worth living, and your
belief will help create that fact.
William James

Life is like an onion: you peel it off one layer at a time, and
sometimes you weep.
Karl Sandburg

Go out on a limb, that's where the fruit is.
Jimmy Carter

Make the most of life while you may
Life is short and wears away!
William Oldys

Remember the sun always rises and sets
Even when the clouds drift over and hide its face.
Jackie Arnold

There are only two ways to live your life,
One is as though nothing is a miracle,
The other is as though everything is a miracle.
Albert Einstein

Love

Love is patient, love is kind. It does not envy, it does not boast, it is not proud. It is not rude, it is not self-seeking, it is not easily angered, it keeps no record of wrongs. Love does not delight in evil but rejoices with the truth. It always protects, always trusts, always hopes, always perseveres. Love never fails.
Corinthians 13: 4–8

Place me like a seal over your heart, like a seal on your arm; for love is as strong as death, its jealousy unyielding as the grave. It burns like a blazing fire, like a mighty flame. Many waters cannot quench love; rivers cannot wash it away. If one were to give all the wealth of his house for love, it would be utterly scorned.
Song of Songs 2.16

Love does not begin and end the way we seem to think it does. Love is a battle, love is a war; love is a growing up.
James Baldwin

Love is a fire. But whether it is going to warm your heart or burn down your house, you can never tell.
Joan Crawford

A toast to you because:

You, yourself, as much as anybody in the entire universe, deserve your love and affection.
Buddha

We've got this gift of love, but love is like a precious plant. You can't just accept it and leave it in the cupboard or just think it's going to get on by itself. You've got to keep watering it. You've got to really look after it and nurture it.
John Lennon

Love, free as air, at sight of human ties
Spreads his light wings, and in a moment flies
Alexander Pope

A toast to the (absent) love of the human race:

I wish I loved the human race
I wish I loved its silly face
I wish I liked the way it walks
I wish I liked the way it talks
And when I'm introduced to one
I wish I thought what jolly fun!
Grumpy old man – Sir Walter Raleigh

We always believe our first love is our last
And our last love our first.
Melville Whyte

The only way to get rid of temptation is to yield to it. And….
I can resist everything except temptation.
Oscar Wilde

Luck

A handful of trumps a road with no bumps
Good luck in your work and your play
Good bottle of wine, friends round to dine
Let's hope this luck stays from today.
Jackie Arnold

May we never forget the privilege of good luck.
Jackie Arnold

May you be merry and lack nothing.
(Shakespeare)

Men

Men are like wine: some turn to vinegar,
but the best improve with age.
Pope John XXIII

Here's to the men! Let's toast them!
And freely admit we love them!
We love them all, be they short or tall
So here's to the men, we toast them!

Pretty girl in your fast car,
He's a wondering where you are;
He's just thinking what he'd do,
If he could just catch up with you
Kiss you once kiss you twice,
Oh yes, he thinks, would that be nice!
Jackie Arnold

To Man – He's the only animal that laughs, drinks when he's
not thirsty, and makes love at all seasons of the year.
Voltaire

Money

It is unwise to pay too much but it is worse to pay too little. When you pay too much, you lose a little money ... that is all, when you pay too little, you sometimes lose everything, because the thing/service you bought was incapable of doing the things it was bought to do.
John Ruskin

A toast to money for:

If we had no winter, the spring would not be so pleasant; If we did not sometimes taste of adversity, prosperity would not be so welcome.
Anne Bradstreet

Don't ever underestimate the importance of money. I know it has often been said that money won't make you happy, and this is undeniably true, but everything else being equal, it's a lovely thing to have around the house.
Groucho Marx

Money is like manure; it's not worth a thing unless it's spread around encouraging young things to grow.
Thornton Wilder

New Year's Eve

*The first glass for thirst
The second for nourishment
The third for pleasure
The fourth for embarrassment.*

Here's to the present.
The hell with the past!
A health to the future, and joy to the last!

In the new year, may your right hand
always be stretched out in friendship,
but never in want.

May you look back on the past
with as much pleasure as you look forward to the future.

Here's a toast to the future, a toast to the past.
And a toast to our friends, far and near.
May the future be pleasant, the past a bright dream.
May our friends remain faithful and dear.

Here's to the bright New Year, and a fond farewell to the old;
here's to the things that are yet to come, and to the memories
that we hold.

Openings

The object of opening the mind, as of opening the mouth,
Is to shut it again on something solid.
G.K. Chesterton

A toast to originality:

The principle mark of genius is not perfection but originality,
the opening of new frontiers.
Arthur Koestler

Revolution

You can never have a revolution in order to establish a democracy.
You must have a democracy to establish a revolution.
G.K. Chesterton

Revolutions have never lightened the burden of tyranny
They have only shifted it to another shoulder.
George Bernard Shaw

When dictatorship is a fact revolution becomes a right.
Victor Hugo

Revolutions are not about trifles but they spring from trifles.
Aristotle

Stress

They say stress is a killer but I think no stress is equally deadly,
especially as you get older. If your days just seem to skip by
without any highs or lows, without some anxieties and pulse-
quickening occurrences, you may not really be living.
Helen Hayes

Time

Times goes you say? Ah no!
Alas, times stays, we go.
Henry Austin Dobson

Lost yesterday, somewhere between sunrise and sunset, two golden
hours each set with sixty diamond minutes. No reward is offered
for they are gone forever.
Horace Mann

Wanted – two hours of heightened awareness where being is accepted while not doing or saying anything and where the present is as it should be now.
Jackie Arnold

Time is a companion that goes with us on a journey. It reminds us to cherish each moment, because it will never come again. What we leave behind is not as important as how we have lived.
From the film *Star Trek Generations*

Procrastination is the thief of time.
Edward Young

Wine

Good days are to be gathered like sunshine in grapes
To be trodden and bottled into wine and kept for age to sip at ease beside the fire.
If the traveller has vintaged well, he need not trouble to wander any longer,
The ruby moments glow in his glass at will.
Freya Stark

Drink wine and live here merry while you may
Tomorrow's life is far too late – live for today.
James M. McLean

Give some wine to your friends
Accept wine they offer to you
Toast to life and friendship
Today and all year through.
Jackie Arnold

Winning

Success can make you go one of two ways. It can make you a prima donna, or it can smooth the edges, take away the insecurities, let the nice things come out.
Barbara Walters

Champions aren't made in gyms. Champions are made from something they have deep inside them – a desire, a dream, a vision. They have to have the skill, and the will. But the will must be stronger than the skill.
Muhammad Ali

You must live in the present, launch yourself on every wave, find your eternity in each moment. Fools stand on their island of opportunities and look toward another land. There is no other land; there is no other life but this.
Henry David Thoreau

Wisdom

I hope our wisdom will grow with our power, and teach us, that the less we use our power the greater it will be.
Thomas Jefferson

Happiness is a butterfly, which, when pursued, is always just beyond your grasp, but which, if you will sit down quietly, may alight upon you.
Nathaniel Hawthorne

In the path of our happiness shall we find the learning for which we have chosen this lifetime.
Richard Bach

There are two things to aim at in life:
First to get what you want and after that to enjoy it.
Only the wisest of mankind achieve the second.
Logan Smith

I shall be like that tree, I shall die at the top.
Jonathan Swift

One of the greatest handicaps is to fear a mistake. You have
stopped yourself. You have to move freely into the arena, not
just to wait for the perfect situation, the perfect moment…
If you have to make a mistake it is better to make a mistake
of action than one of inaction.
If I had the opportunity again I would take chances.
Frederico Fellini

It's a funny thing about life,
if you refuse to accept anything but the best,
you very often get it.
W. Somerset Maugham

Women

Remember, Ginger Rogers did everything Fred Astaire did,
but she did it backwards and in high heels.
Faith Wittlesey

The secret of staying young is to live honestly, eat slowly
And lie about your age.
Lucille Ball

I have everything now that I had twenty years ago
Except now it's all lower.
Gypsy Rose Lee

I like living
I have sometimes been wildly, despairingly, acutely miserable,
racked with sorrow.
But through it all I still know that just to be alive is a grand
thing.
Agatha Christie

From one of the greatest women of all time:

We ourselves feel that what we are doing is just a drop in the
ocean. But if that drop was not in the ocean, I think that ocean
would be less because of that missing drop.
Mother Teresa

Toasts for the Trades

The baker:

To he who loafs around all day and still makes the dough!

The butcher:

To the one who always gets to the heart of (or down to the
bones of) the matter.
His cut is always the deepest!

The blacksmith:

The one who always forges his way to victory.

The carpet fitter:

Who makes a 'pile' of money and is never 'stuck' for words.

The cook:

He/she always has his/her cake and eats it!
The angry cook whose pans fly by
But he feeds us well, you and I!

The decorator:

Who is always up against it and still remains stuck up!

The firefighter:

The army that draws water not blood and thanks instead of tears.

The fisherman:

The steady fisherman who never 'reels' home
May the holes in your net be no bigger than your fish.
Irish

The glazier:

Who takes panes to see his way through life.

The grocer:

Whose honest tea is the best policy
May our hearts never be hard like those of cabbages,
nor may we be rotten at the core.

The hairdresser:

May he/she never be hacked off with us.
They help keep us in trim, always in style but never at a snip!

The jeweller:

He/she never loses his/her sparkle.
Whose diamonds are always a girl's best friend.

The journalist:

Who has the tongue of the country – may it never be cut out!

The lawyer:

Who rescues your estate from your enemies, and keeps it
himself! However, you cannot live without them and you
certainly cannot die without them!

The locksmith:

Who holds the key to everyone's heart.

The mechanic:

Who often takes a 'brake' and is therefore seldom 'exhaust'ed.

The milliner:

They often keep things under their hat but never talk through it.

The optician:

He/she will always see the world through rose-tinted lenses but will seldom prescribe them.
Whose focus is always clear and who will never cross a bridge before they come to them.

The painter:

He/she leads a colourful life, always has a different perspective and is the only one able to 'still' life.

The rubbish collector:

Who never 'wastes' a moment and whose mind is completely uncluttered.

The shoemaker:

They have leathery faces, are good 'souls' and are never down on their uppers.

The tailor:

Who often gives you short measure but will never cut the bill!

The undertaker:

May they never overtake us, under-estimate us but always let us down!

The vet:

Who will always let sleeping dogs lie, never let the cat out of the bag and can sometimes be seen taking the horse to water and making it drink!

The waiter:

Who is always waiting for his starter for ten!

8. Proverbs and Limericks

This book is about toasts, quotes and short speeches and although proverbs do not come under this heading I felt it would be useful to include some here. When we make a short speech it is nice to drop a proverb in to liven it up and to underline the meaning. Here are some useful ones in alphabetical order for ease of use.

A

Ask no questions and you will be told no lies   18th cent

B

Better a little fire to warm us than a great
one to burn us   16th cent
Better be born lucky than rich   J. Clarke
Better to go to bed supperless than rise in debt   J. Ray Better
Be a friend to yourself and others will be a friend to you   J. Kelly
Better the devil you know than the devil you don't   19th cent
Better the foot slip than the tongue   16th cent

C

Content lives more often in cottages than in palaces   T. Fuller
Courtesy on one side only doesn't last long   G. Herbert
Creditors have better memories than debtors   J. Howell

D

Do as I say not as I do   J. Heywood
Do not do all you can, spend all you have,
believe all you hear, and tell all you know.   H.G. Bohn

| Do not meet troubles halfway | 16th cent |
| Do not put all your eggs in one basket | 18th cent |

E

Early to bed, early to rise makes a man healthy wealthy and wise	16th cent
Eat at pleasure drink by measure	French
Eat to live but do not live to eat	Latin
Every cloud has a silver lining	19th cent
Every little helps	18th cent
Everyone is the architect of his/her own fortune	Latin
Every white has its black and every sweet its sour	18th cent
Extreme right is extreme wrong	Latin

F

Far from the eye far from the heart	13th cent
Fearful heart never won a fair lady	16th cent
Few words are best	16th cent
First think then speak	J. Clarke
Follow the river and you'll get to the sea	T. Fuller
Forewarned is forearmed	Latin
Friendships multiply joy and divide grief	H. G. Bohn

G

Give a lie twenty-four hours start and you can never overtake it	V. S. Lean
Good advice is beyond price	Latin
Good words cost nothing	16th cent

H

| He cannot speak well that cannot hold his tongue | 17th cent |
| He is not a wise man who cannot play the fool on occasion | 16th cent |

He laughs best that laughs last	18th cent
He that borrows must pay with shame or loss	J. Ray
He that falls today may rise tomorrow	17th cent
He who has time and looks for time, loses time	16th cent
Health is better than wealth	16th cent
Hear, see and be still	15th cent
History repeats itself	19th cent
Honesty is the best policy	16th cent
Honey in the mouth saves the purse	Italian

I

I cannot be your friend and your flatterer too	17th cent
I say little but think more	15th cent
I will not make a toil of pleasure	17th cent
Idleness makes the wit rust	T. Fuller
If I had not lifted up the stone you would not have found the jewel	J. Ray
If money is not your servant it will be your master	17th cent
If you put nothing in your purse you can take nothing out	T. Fuller
It is easy to be wise after the event	17th cent

K

Keep your mouth shut and your eyes wide open	18th cent
Kindle not a fire that you cannot extinguish	16th cent

L

Late repentance is seldom true	Latin
Life is half spent before we know what it is	G. Herbert
Life would be too smooth if it had no runs in it	T. Fuller
Like a fish out of water	Latin
Like a red rag to a bull	16th cent
Like water off a duck's back	19th cent
Little strokes fell great oaks	16th cent

Little things please little minds	Latin
Lose an hour in the morning and you'll be all day hunting for it	19th cent
Love comes in at the window and goes out at the door	W. Camdon
Love does much but money does all	French
Love will find a way	16th cent

M

Make hay while the sun shines	J. Heywood
Many a true word is spoken in jest (fun)	14th cent
Marry first and love will follow	17th cent
Marry in haste repent at leisure	16th cent
Milk says to wine – welcome friend	G. Herbert

N

Never ask pardon before you are accused	H. G. Bohn
Never cast dirt into that fountain where you have drunk	J. Ray
Never cross a bridge until you come to it	19th cent
Never put off till tomorrow what may be done today	14th cent
Never venture out of your depth until you can swim	H. G. Bohn
No sunshine but it has some shadow	J. Ray
No time like the present	17th cent
No wisdom like silence	Greek
None so blind as those who won't see	16th cent
None so deaf as those who won't hear	16th cent
Nothing is impossible to a willing heart	J. Heywood

O

Old friends and old wine are best	T. Draxe
One day of pleasure is worth two of sorrow	T. Fuller
One half of the world does not know how the other half lives	G. Herbert
One hour today is worth two tomorrow	T. Fuller

One hour's sleep before midnight is worth two after   G. Herbert
One man's meat is another man's poison   Latin
One must draw the line somewhere   19th cent
One pair of legs is worth two pairs of hands   16th cent
Opportunity makes the thief   13th cent
Out of sight, out of mind   13th cent
Out of the frying pan, into the fire   J. Heywood

P

Patience is a flower that does not grow in every garden   J. Heywood
Pigs might fly but they are very unlikely birds   19th cent
Practise makes perfect   Latin
Prevention is better than cure   Latin
Pride goes before and shame follows after   14th cent
Punctuality is the soul of business   H.G. Bohn
Put that in your pipe and smoke it   19th cent

R

Rain before seven fine before eleven   19th cent
Remove an old tree and it will die   16th cent
Respect a man and he will do more   J. Howell
Ride softly that you may get home sooner   J. Ray
Rome was not built in a day   Latin
Rule youth well for age will rule itself   D. Fergusson

S

Save your breath to cool your porridge   16th cent
Say as men say but think to yourself   J. Clarke
Say well is good but do well is better   J. Clarke
Scratch my back and I'll scratch yours   19 cent
Silence seldom does harm   J. Ray
Six of one and half a dozen of the other   19th cent
Some are wise and some are otherwise   J. Howell
Sometimes the best gain is to lose   G. Herbert

Speech is the picture of the mind	J. Ray
Sticks and stones may break my bones but words will never hurt me	19th cent
Still waters run deep	19th cent
Stolen pleasures are sweetest	17th cent
Strike while the iron is hot	14th cent
Sweep before your own door	17th cent

T

Take care of the pence and the pounds will take care of them selves	18th cent
Take time while time is, for time flies away	16th cent
That is an empty purse if full of another's money	Latin
The best mirror is an old friend	J. Ray
The day has eyes the night has ears	D. Fergusson
The early bird catches the worm	W. Camden
The end justifies the means	17th cent
The higher up the greater the fall	16th cent
The morning hour has gold in its mouth	German
The remedy for injuries is not to remember them	Italian
The remedy for love is – land between	Spanish
The stone that lies not in your way need not offend you	T. Fuller
The way to an Englishman's heart is through his stomach	19th cent
The way to be safe is never to feel secure	T. Fuller
The world is his who enjoys it	18th cent
There is no general rule without some exception	17th cent
Think much, speak little, write less	Italian
Time and tide wait for no man	16th cent
Time is money	18th cent
Times change and we change with them	Latin
Truth looks for no corners and never grows old	16th cent

U

Under the blanket black is as good as white	T. Fuller
Unlucky in love, lucky at play	18th cent

V

Variety is the spice of life	17th cent
Vice makes virtue shine	T. Fuller
Vows made in storms are forgotten in calms	T. Fuller

W

Walls have ears	17th cent
Waste not want not	18th cent
We are born crying, live complaining and die disappointed	T. Fuller
We can live without our friends, not without our neighbours	J. Kelly
We leave more to do when we die, than we have done	G. Herbert
We never miss the water till the well runs dry	J. Kelly
Well begun is half done	Italian
What costs little is little esteemed	17th cent
What greater crime than loss of time	T. Fuller
What is worth doing is worth doing well	19th cent
What the eye doesn't see the heart doesn't grieve over	19th cent
When fortune knocks open the door	17th cent
When in Rome do as the Romans do	Latin
When one door shuts another one opens	Spanish
When the cat's away the mice will play	16th cent
Who does not keep a penny will never have many	J. Clarke
Who lives by hope will die by hunger	Italian
Without danger we cannot get beyond danger	G. Herbert
Words cut more than swords	13th cent

Y

Years know more than books	G. Herbert
Yesterday will not be called again	16th cent
You cannot have your cake and eat it	J. Heywood
You cannot get blood (or water) out of a stone	Latin
You cannot know wine by the barrel	G. Herbert
You cannot lose what you never had	17th cent
You cannot see the wood for the trees	J. Heywood
You may take a horse to water but you can't make him drink	J. Heywood
You must look where it is not as well as where it is	T. Fuller
You never know what you can do till you try	19th cent
You pays your money and you takes your choice	V.S. Lean

Z

Zeal without knowledge is fire without light	T. Fuller
Zeal without prudence is frenzy	T. Fuller

Limericks

Limericks originated from the place called Limerick in Ireland. They are often frowned upon as being bawdy and used only by drunks, however they can be very useful as they are easy to make up and can be funny. Why not give them a go? They could enhance any toast or short speech.

How to make up your own limerick

Lines one, two, and five of limericks have seven to ten syllables and rhyme with one another. Lines three and four of limericks have five to seven syllables and also rhyme with each other.

This is one of the most famous limericks by Edward Lear.

> There was an Old Man with a beard,
> Who said, 'It is just as I feared!
> Two Owls and a Hen,
> Four Larks and a Wren,
> Have all built their nests in my beard!'

Build your own limericks like this:

There was a:

1. ... *Young man from Seaford*

2. ... *Young lady from Kent*

Who said:

1. ... *He was going abroad*

2. ... *All her money was spent*

Then put in two short rhyming lines like this:

1. *He packed up his case*
Said 'I'm leaving this place'

2. *She started to sing*
Wore masses of bling

Then add the last line to rhyme with the first and second.

1. *Now he owns a French chateau – my lord!*

2. *She now lives with a millionaire gent!*

The results are:

1. *There was a young man from Sea*ford
*Who said he was going ab*road
He picked up his case
Said I'm leaving this place
Now he owns a French chateau – my lord!

2. *There was a young lady from Kent*
Who said all her money was spent
She started to sing
Wore masses of bling
She now lives with a millionaire gent!

———

If you want to make it even more original you can match it to your special occasion. Try making up your own. Here are some examples:

Anniversary

We've been on this road many years
Done the heartache, shed the tears
Now let's forget
No longer regret
I'll pour the wine, darling – cheers!

Business success

This year has been tough on the line
You've met all your targets and mine!
You all pulled as one
Well, I did load the gun!
So let's fill up those glasses with wine!

Good luck for someone leaving

You're leaving to find pastures new
We will miss all the things that you do
But good luck on your way
We really must say
Now let's raise our glasses to you!

Graduation or successful school year

The hours spent slogging away
The times we have called it a day
You stayed up at night
Till the owls all took flight
Celebrate your success – yes, I'd say!

Wedding

Tom's getting married in spring
He's given his lady a ring
Let's toast him today
And let us all say
May your marriage much happiness bring!

9. Workbook

Speech Samples

Useful introductions at semi-formal and informal occasions:

Friends/colleagues/ladies and gentlemen

If you are not able to make yourself heard initially, just stand and wait for silence.

Introductions

• Please can I have your attention for a few moments …

• May I ask you to 'lend me your ears' …

• I'd like to say a few words on this special occasion …

• May I ask you to raise your glasses to … (name)

• I would like to propose a toast to … (name)

• May I take this opportunity to offer a toast to … (name)

• It gives me great pleasure to propose a toast to … (name)

• On this happy occasion I would like to offer a toast to … (name)

• In fond memory of (name) I would like to propose a toast …

• Congratulations to (name/s) on this wonderful achievement/occasion …

A model for structuring your speech – S.T.A.R.T

S – stop (your negative thoughts and focus on your strengths and personal qualities)

T – think (about your audience and find out about them/him/her)

A – ask (yourself and others what kind of quotes/stories/toasts would make an impact)

R – reflect (on your three main points and weave in stories/anecdotes)

T – trust (your own brain and your ability to be a success – then practise)

The mini speech Planning Wheel:

Use the wheel to think of topics for your mini speech

What did you find out about the people/person you are addressing? Add these to the wheel

Then select those points that naturally link together

Begin to group ideas and structure your introduction main text and conclusion

Ideas for Main Body of Text

During the planning stage of your toast/short speech think about the person you are going to aim your toast/speech at.

• What do you know about their life?

_____

_____

_____

• Who could you ask for information on this person?

_____

_____

• Are there any photos you could use to jog your memory? Y/N

• What unusual pastimes/hobbies does this person have?

_____

_____

• Do they have any funny habits?

_____

_____

• Are there any unusual phrases they always say?

_____

_____

- What are they interested in, eg pets, music, travel, fashion, sport, art, collecting?

_____

_____

- After you have done some background research collect this information and decide how you will weave it into your speech.

- Can you find a quote, toast or proverb in the book that would complement any of the information?

_____

- What visual prop (photo, article of clothing, item connected to an unusual hobby or interest) could be shown to the audience in connection with this speech?

_____

- Could you bring a CD/DVD or piece of music that would make people laugh (but not embarrass the person)?

_____

- Has this person done anything really successful, remarkable or interesting in his/her life?

_____

_____

- Can you include any startling facts or unusual moments in connection with this area of their life?

_____

- What else happened on the day they were born? Can you include a little story that would enhance the toast/speech?

_____

_____

Endings/Conclusion

End your speech with a quote or short story and your toast by saying one of the following:

So, let's raise our glasses to (name). Cheers!

So, many thanks from us all to (name). Cheers!

Well, I would now like to propose a toast to (name). Cheers!
To your health!

Let's raise our glasses to everyone here!
(Clink your glass with your neighbours on both sides)

Or choose from the many toasts, quotes, proverbs
and limericks in this book!

10. The Five Steps to Successful Speaking and the Fifty Tips to Get You There

Step one – Facing the fears

1. Know that fear makes you sharper and heightens your reflexes.

2. Understand that fear usually occurs before you speak – convert it to excitement and it will disappear as you get into your stride.

3. Use visualisation to 'see' yourself giving a successful and interesting toast/speech. (Do this every evening for at least a week before your event.)

4. Close your eyes and imagine the audience listening and applauding.

5. Concentrate on what you do well.

6. Practise what you feel is a challenge – use a mirror and ask your friends.

7. Think about your desire to help and inform the audience – it's not about you.

8. If you memorise your opening and closing, the middle will take care of itself!

9. Arrive on time and meet as many friendly faces as possible.

10. Imagine you are talking to a group of your friends – 'see' them in the audience.

Step two – Make it easy on yourself

1. You are a unique person – just be yourself and know that the best speakers are not performers.

2. Practise by speaking your toast/script onto a tape and listening to it in your car/home.

3. Banish the butterflies by doing some form of physical exercise just before you begin.

4. Be comfortable with your appearance and then forget about it.

5. Try to visit the venue before you speak to get a feel for the room.

6. Check your equipment/props in advance both before and at the event. It is too late five minutes before you begin.

7. Banish the 'it will not go well' voices by visualising yourself giving a very successful and well-organised speech/toast. Do this on a regular basis.

8. Organise your notes well. Clip them together and number them in reverse order. (The latter is a great motivator as you know exactly how many to the end!)

9. Plan your structure – use colour codes for the three key points.

10. Ask yourself 'what else can I do to really make this as easy/enjoyable as possible?'

Step three – Preparation

1. Brainstorm – take a sheet of paper and jot down your ideas. Go with the flow and let your mind play with thoughts and ideas.

2. Use a list, spider-graph or a mind-map to help organise them.

3. Underline the three top ideas that really appeal to you.

4. Select the most interesting/relevant topic for your audience and put down all your thoughts around the topic you have chosen.

5. Select a quote or toast that fits the occasion.

6. Ask yourself questions with what and where and when, how and why and who, eg:

   What are my objectives?
   Where can I get further information about my toastee?
   When do I need to have the first draft ready?
   How can I be sure I am giving something of value
       to the toastee?
   Why will this topic/toast work best?
   Who will be happy with/offended by my toast?
   List your own 'open' questions.

7. Write the answers so that you can use them as a tool every time you address an audience.

8. Write the first draft of your speech keeping to the three main points.

9. Summarise it onto numbered index cards.

10. Practise and time it, in front of a mirror/family.

Step four – Voice

1. Practise breathing from the diaphragm.

2. Hold your breath for at least sixty seconds to increase your lung capacity (build up slowly).

3. Hum to yourself – this increases the flexibility of the vocal cords and aids projection.

4. Use stress to emphasise important words in your delivery.

5. Pause after the stressed word for the audience to absorb it.

6. Change your pace during the delivery (mark it on your notes).

7. Concentrate on voice tone – where can you speak in a lower or higher tone? (Write this on your notes.)

8. Pause and breathe during your delivery – the audience also need to!

9. Stand upright and drop your shoulders allowing your neck and throat to be free of restriction.

10. Trust your own voice to come from within – no force, just natural flow.

Step five – External resources

1. Time, it's a short speech! Take a small travel clock with you and place it where you can see it.

2. Ask someone in the audience to give you a sign when you are two minutes from the end.

3. Keep within the time – never exceed it.

4. Be a 'speaker' not a 'reader' – try to keep notes to a minimum.

5. If you need notes put them on small cards you can hold in your hand.

6. Link them together with a clip/ring so they can't fall and get mixed up!

7. Present props and show photos so that everyone can see them.

8. Prepare your props so that they are in front of you and you don't need to turn your back.

9. Make sure there is a glass of water on the table near you.

10. Ensure you can see your notes clearly and that there is plenty of light.

Good luck.

Resources

I would like to thank the following contributors.

In particular Trish Lambert of 4-R Marketing for her excellent research and for her knowledge and support.

My daughters Catherine, Martina and Petra and many friends who gave me tips and toasts they had heard or made up!

Daniella Horder, John Postlethwaite, John Howell, Alex Marshall, Sharon Statt, David Robertson and my colleague Alison Haill of Oxford Professional English.

The students and staff of the English Language Centre in Brighton.

Reference Books

A Brief History of the Raised Glass, Paul Dickson
Extraordinary Origins of Everyday Things, Charles Panati
The Complete Book of Toasts, Paul Dickson
The Everyman Dictionary of Quotations and Proverbs, Compiled by D.C. Browning

Internet

If you put into Google the word 'Toasts' you will be guided to a host of websites on the internet that are often very useful and amusing – do check for copyright, but most will allow toasts to be used for non-commercial purposes.

Other websites:

www.coach4executives.com – for business/executive coaching and cross-cultural understanding

www.toastmasters.org.uk – to join a toastmaster speakers club

Index

John Bowden

Making the Best Man's Speech

This is a guide for prospective best men which aims to answer the anxieties about making the speech. It offers advice on speech-making essentials, great openings, strong middles, big finishes, plus putting it all together and delivering the speech itself.

Making the Father of the Bride's Speech

You have a wonderful opportunity to add to the magic of your daughter's wedding. Your words will linger in memories – they may even be captured on film for future generations to hear. So what are the golden rules of speech-making? How can you convey emotion, seriousness and add a touch of humour?

Making the Bridegroom's Speech

What are the golden rules of speech making? How should you respond to the toast to the bride and groom? And which people do you need to thank and how? The answers to all these questions and more are here in this much-needed book. Now you can make your wedding day speech memorable for all the right reasons! Add sincerity, sparkle and humour, and best of all, enjoy the big day.

VAUGHAN EVANS

STAND, SPEAK, DELIVER!

HOW TO SURVIVE AND THRIVE IN PUBLIC SPEAKING AND PRESENTING

Stand, Speak, Deliver!

How to survive and thrive in public speaking and presenting

Vaughn Evans

Available to buy in ebook and paperback

'There is a real danger that this book will turn public
speaking into something that you can actually enjoy.'
Graham Davies, speaker and author of
The Presentation Coach

Public speaking and presenting rank in the top ten of
people's greatest fears. Yet being able to speak coherently and
persuasively in a speech, seminar or meeting room is
important when progressing our careers and living our lives
to the fullest.

In this book, 37 short, lively and pithy speeches tell us how
to construct and deliver a speech or presentation. Each
speech follows a simple, perfect structure which will soon
become imprinted in your mind.

Stand, Speak, Deliver! will enable you to learn how to
use your eyes, vary your voice and move your body. It will
also look at how to inform, entertain, humour, persuade,
motivate or inspire the audience; how to present, to
colleagues or clients; how to introduce a speaker;
and how to wow as best man.

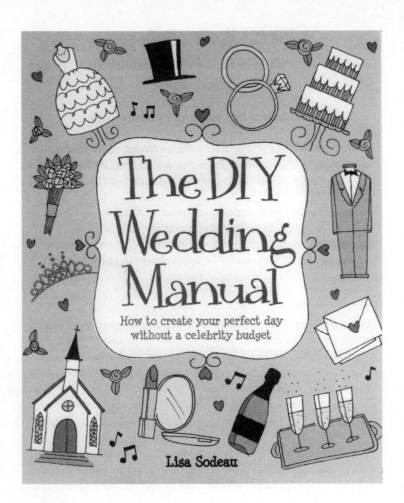

The DIY Wedding Manual

How to create your perfect day
without a celebrity budget

Lisa Sodeau

The DIY Wedding Manual
How to create your perfect day without a celebrity budget

Lisa Sodeau

Available to buy in ebook and paperback

This book will show you that with a little bit of planning and preparation, it is possible to have the day of your dreams without starting married life in debt.

The average cost of a wedding is about as much as a deposit on a house, but one thing the 'credit crunch' taught us all is that there are many areas in our lives where we can save money by doing things ourselves. So why should weddings be an exception?

Whether it's boom or bust you don't have to spend a fortune. You really can create your own special day by doing it yourself and having fun along the way. This book is packed with top tips and money saving ideas for: Stationery, Venues, Flowers, Transport, Hair and Make-up, Photographs, Food and Drink, the Reception and much more – including tips from real-life brides and more than 100 budget busting ideas.